The Gospel
According *to the* Trinity

The Gospel According *to the* Trinity

*How the Doctrine of the Trinity Impacts
Redemption from Eternity to Eternity*

Nicholas S. Perez

WIPF *&* STOCK · Eugene, Oregon

THE GOSPEL ACCORDING TO THE TRINITY
How the Doctrine of the Trinity Impacts Redemption from Eternity to Eternity

Copyright © 2025 Nicholas S. Perez. All rights reserved. Except for brief quotations in critical publications or reviews, no part of this book may be reproduced in any manner without prior written permission from the publisher. Write: Permissions, Wipf and Stock Publishers, 199 W. 8th Ave., Suite 3, Eugene, OR 97401.

Wipf & Stock
An Imprint of Wipf and Stock Publishers
199 W. 8th Ave., Suite 3
Eugene, OR 97401

www.wipfandstock.com

PAPERBACK ISBN: 979-8-3852-3795-1
HARDCOVER ISBN: 979-8-3852-3796-8
EBOOK ISBN: 979-8-3852-3797-5

VERSION NUMBER 04/18/25

Unless otherwise indicated, all Scripture quotations are from The ESV® Bible (The Holy Bible, English Standard Version®), © 2001 by Crossway, a publishing ministry of Good News Publishers. Used by permission. All rights reserved.

Scripture taken from HOLY BIBLE, NEW INTERNATIONAL VERSION®. Copyright © 1973, 1978, 1984 by International Bible Society. Used by permission of Zondervan Publishing House.

Scripture taken from the NEW AMERICAN STANDARD BIBLE®, Copyright © 1960, 1962, 1963, 1971, 1972, 1973, 1975, 1977, 1995 by The Lockman Foundation. Used by permission.

Scripture quotations taken from the (LSB®) Legacy Standard Bible®, Copyright © 2021 by The Lockman Foundation. Used by permission. All rights reserved. Managed in partnership with Three Sixteen Publishing Inc. LSBible.org and 316publishing.com.

Dedicated to
my family

Contents

List of Table | ix
Preface | xi
List of Abbreviations | xiii

1   The Priority of the Trinity in the Gospel | 1
2   A Single and Harmonious Divine Intention | 7

Part I: Redemption Predestined | 15

3   The Glorification of a People Given by the Father to the Son from Eternity | 17
4   The Choice of a People by the Father in the Son from Eternity | 21
5   The Book of Life | 30

Part II: Redemption Accomplished | 39

6   The Son Offers Himself Through the Spirit to the Father to Obtain Eternal Redemption | 41
7   Propitiation: The Son Satisfies the Father's Wrath | 48

Part III: Redemption Applied | 65

8   The Spirit Gives Life | 67
9   The Spirit Gives Life to Those Given by the Father to the Son | 76
10   The Indwelling, Sanctifying Spirit | 98

Part IV: Redemption Glorified | 107

11　The Glorification of the Redeemed | 109
12　The Golden Chain of Redemption | 113
13　Behold His Glory | 129
14　Putting It All Together | 133

Appendix: Against Universalism | 157
Bibliography | 165
Scripture Index | 169

List of Tables

Table 1—Comparison of Various Possibilities of Outworking of Redemption | 134

Preface

Someone asked me recently, "What made you write this book?" The question caught me by surprise because it had been so long since I first started this project that now that I was at the end of it, I could not immediately recall where it began. I read a lot. So books came to mind (*The Trinity in the Stone-Campbell Movement* and *Jesus in Trinitarian Perspective*, both of which are cited in the pages ahead). The ideas of other authors certainly have a way of sparking other ideas in other people. But then I remembered page one of a notebook with a silver cover, which is written on both sides divided into four sections, which have become the four parts in this book. At the top of the page I had written, "The gospel begins with God."

When discussing the material in this book with people—colleagues, church members, friends, and family—several have commented that what I have done is "start from above." That's accurate. It is also contrary to where many begin. Many presentations of the gospel "start from below," that is, they start with humans: our sin, our great need, our response. We become so focused on "what must I do?" that we miss "what has God done?" This book seeks to focus on the latter.

The other note written on that notebook page is "single divine intention; harmony [within the] Trinity." Trinitarian harmony in the atonement, like what is found in John Owen's writings, started me pursuing trinitarian harmony from eternity to eternity. Texts which had the phrase "before the foundation of the world" or "before time began" were naturally the starting point. Then I moved on from there to the Trinity's actions in time (atonement and sanctification) before landing in eternity future.

These two thoughts—the beginning of the gospel is God and trinitarian harmony in redemption from eternity to eternity—were the genesis of this book. I have sought to make them the primary focus of this work. I have also sought to be as carefully diligent in bringing the reader along the journey. It is admittedly a tall order to go from eternity to eternity following the movements of the Trinity. It can be especially challenging for us in the Restoration Movement, since we have historically eschewed theological language like "Trinity." However, I am hopeful that I can disarm these apprehensions in a chapter or two, so that we can advance further into the discussion.

I do not anticipate this book being popular. Of course I did not anticipate finding a willing publisher, but thankfully it has seen the light of publication courtesy of the kind people at Wipf & Stock. So perhaps my pessimism is unwarranted and unnecessary.

Still, I can't help feeling due to the conclusions I've drawn (from careful examination of the biblical text) that this book will not be well-received. In fact, I anticipate disagreement from certain quarters of the brotherhood. That's fine if you disagree. My appeal to you is simple: answer the arguments. I have sought to be thorough in my exegesis and exposition. I have interacted with the arguments presented against my position found in Restoration Movement literature. I believe that is reflected in the pages ahead. Therefore, if you disagree with the conclusions, I ask that you respond in kind: go to the text of Scripture and show from the text how I am wrong.

Again, I hope I am wrong in my pessimism and this book finds a favorable hearing. No one will be as delighted that this book has been well-received than its author. If it does find such a hearing, it will hopefully mean that the Restoration Movement, and others within broader evangelical Christianity, is aiming at more consistency with how what they believe about the Trinity impacts their understanding of the gospel.

List of Abbreviations

BDAG   Walter Bauer, Frederick W. Danker, W. F. Arndt, and F. W. Gingrich. *Greek-English Lexicon of the New Testament and Other Early Christian Literature.* 3rd ed. Chicago: University of Chicago Press, 2000.

CD   Barth, Karl. *Church Dogmatics.* Translated by G. T. Thomson et al. Edinburgh: T & T Clark, 1936–77.

TDNT   *Theological Dictionary of the New Testament.* 10 vols. Edited by Gerhard Kittel and Gerhard Friedrich. Translated by Geoffrey W. Bromiley. Grand Rapids: Eerdmans, 1964–76.

CHAPTER 1

The Priority of the Trinity in the Gospel

I LOVE THE TRINITY. I love God the Father. I love God the Son. I love God the Holy Spirit. Does this sound strange to you? I have grown up in the churches of Christ my whole life, and I cannot recall once ever hearing a preacher, elder, or member say, "I love the Trinity." Don't get me wrong—I've heard people say, "I love God," or "I love Jesus." I've heard men in prayer pray, "We love you," to our heavenly Father. But I have never heard someone say, "I love the triune God/Trinity."

Yet, we do believe God is three-in-one, i.e., three persons in one being. A typical outworking of the various propositions that comprise the doctrine of the Trinity is as follows:

1. There is only one God (Deut 6:4; Eph 4:6)
2. The Father is true God: Jesus calls the Father "the true God" (John 17:3)
3. The Son is true God: Of "His Son Jesus Christ," the apostle John says, "He is the true God and eternal life" (1 John 5:20)
4. The Holy Spirit is true God: Lying to the Holy Spirit is tantamount to lying to God (Acts 5:3, 4)
5. The Father is *not* the Son: It is the Son standing in the River Jordan, not the Father

6. The Father is *not* the Holy Spirit: It is the Spirit who descends as a dove, not the Father (Matt 3:16–17)

7. The Son is *not* the Holy Spirit: The Son is led by the Spirit (Matt 4:1)[1]

Putting together these various propositions brings into focus the tri-unity of God. One God, three persons.

The Trinity is a doctrine which is derived from careful exegesis of the Scripture. Erickson writes:

> We may say, then, that when the whole text of Scripture is taken seriously, the doctrine of the Trinity emerges. It teaches clearly that God is one and is unique, that he is the only God that is true and exists. It teaches, either directly or indirectly, that there are three persons who are fully divine, the Father, the Son, and the Holy Spirit. And it also teaches, indirectly and by implication, that these three are one.[2]

The key phrases in Erickson's statement are concerning the Scriptures teaching "clearly," "either directly or indirectly," and "indirectly and by implication." Feinberg accentuates the implied nature of the doctrine of the Trinity when he writes, "While no passage states the doctrine *per se*, there are other ways Scripture can teach something. If Scripture makes various claims which, when taken together, necessitate or even warrant a doctrine, then the Bible teaches the doctrine by implication."[3] So it is with the doctrine of the Trinity. Thus, Sanders writes, "The doctrine of the Trinity is a vast doctrinal complex containing numerous ideas, summarizing vast stretches of biblical revelation, integrating them, and holding them together so they can be taken in at one mental glance."[4] Scripture teaches the above seven propositions either clearly, directly, or indirectly. Then, taken together, it can be said that the Scriptures teach *by implication* the doctrine of the Trinity. The Trinity is not *explicitly* stated or taught in the Scriptures.

---

1. Feinberg provides these seven propositions (*No One Like Him*, 438); I have fleshed them out briefly. Numerous authors have documented these several propositions which comprise the doctrine of the Trinity. E.g., see Warfield, "Trinity," 3016; Erickson, *Making Sense of the Trinity*, 17–42; Boice, *Foundations*, 113–16, sets forth the doctrine in five propositions; Sanders summarizes the propositions in paragraph format, explaining that the propositions can be formulated in as few as three and as many as nine points (*Triune God*, 173).

2. Erickson, *Making Sense of the Trinity*, 42.

3. Feinberg, *No One Like Him*, 443. Emphasis original.

4. Sanders, *Triune God*, 172–73.

Warfield summarizes the point nicely, "The doctrine of the Trinity is given to us in Scripture, not in formulated definition, but in fragmentary allusions; when we assemble the *disjecta membra* [i.e., scattered fragments] into their organic unity, we are not passing from Scripture, but entering more thoroughly into the meaning of Scripture."[5] Therefore, a consistent exegesis of the entire biblical witness warrants faith in the triune God.

One text which captures the unity and trinity within the Godhead is the Great Commission: "Go, therefore, and make disciples of all nations, baptizing them in the Name of the Father, and of the Son, and of the Holy Spirit, etc" (Matt 28:19). There is threeness—the three persons mentioned: Father, Son, and Holy Spirit. But there is oneness—a singular name unites the three persons. Is there a word which conveys this three-in-oneness which, while not found in Scripture, carries the weight of the seven (7) propositions above? Indeed, "Trinity" is just such a word.

The Trinity is without doubt both a doctrine revealed in Scripture and a doctrine to be believed. However, few Christians go the next step in determining the practical significance that the doctrine of the Trinity has upon their lives. We in the churches of Christ are no exception. Specifically, how does the doctrine of the Trinity impact the gospel? This book is aimed at answering this question.

The doctrine of the Trinity has serious implications for the gospel. At the end of his book on the Trinity, James White draws attention to how the doctrine of the Trinity impacts the gospel. He writes, "The Gospel, as it is proclaimed in Scripture, is Trinitarian. Remove the Father and you have no Gospel. Remove the Son and the Gospel ceases to exist. Remove the Spirit, and the Gospel has no existence."[6] Feinberg identifies how this is so by pointing out that the Savior of sinful humanity could not be a mere human but must be fully God. "If Jesus is less than God," asks Feinberg, "how can he serve as the atoning sacrifice?"[7] Jesus cannot satisfy the wrath of God the Father if he is not God. Further, if the Holy Spirit is not fully God there is no way one can be certain that he will regenerate, apply the completed work of Christ to, and indwell the believer.[8] Without the Trinity, God does not send God to be the Savior of the World. Without the Trinity, God does not send God into our hearts (Gal 4:6). Without the Trinity there is no gospel.

---

5. Warfield, "Trinity," 3012.
6. White, *Forgotten Trinity*, 194.
7. Feinberg, *No One Like Him*, 440.
8. Feinberg, *No One Like Him*, 440.

The Priority of the Trinity in the Gospel

AVOIDING THE TRINITY

Despite the reality that without the Trinity there is no gospel, the Stone-Campbell Movement has had a delicate, even tenuous relationship with the Trinity. In his book *The Trinity in the Stone-Campbell Movement*, Kelly Carter shows how a deliberate choice was made by the Campbells (more so Alexander than Thomas) and Stone to avoid Trinitarian language, resulting in Stone espousing nearly heterodox views on the deity of the Son. Summarizing, Carter writes:

> The history of thought within [Independent Christian Churches/Churches of Christ and Churches of Christ (a capella)] demonstrates that the [Stone-Campbell Movement] has generally been orthodox Trinitarian in its theological orientation. Although there have been exceptions, Restorationists have typically been Trinitarian, albeit hesitant to use traditional Trinitarian language and speculative argumentation, especially when it contributes to disunity between Christians... [Explicitly] Trinitarian doctrine has not been a shaping force of doctrine and practice.[9]

Carter concludes that Stone-Campbell churches are typically Trinitarian, even orthodox Trinitarian. Yet, the same churches are not overtly Trinitarian, hesitant to use the traditional Trinitarian language which has developed historically. For example, those in the Restoration Movement have tended to shy away from terms like "person," "substance/essence," and "Trinity," since such terms are not in the Bible. Compounding the predicament is the relative dearth of material produced by Restoration Movement authors. Carter documents just three works produced in the 20th century by Restoration Movement authors, only two of which are specifically on the Trinity.

This insight helps put into context some of the controversies within the Restoration Movement through the years. For example, in the late 1980s and early 1990s, Wayne Jackson and Gary Workman engaged in a written debate over whether a Christian could pray to Jesus.[10] Workman (and others) argued that one prays *to* the Father *through* Jesus. Jackson, citing biblical and historical precedence, argued that Christ is a proper object of worship including prayer. Such a controversy only has legs because of the deliberate trajectory set by the early Restoration Movement leaders'

---

9. Carter, *Trinity*, 218–19.

10. Jackson, "Praying to Jesus," 16–29, documents from his vantage point the nexus of and his involvement with this controversy.

avoidance of Trinitarian language. The debate ends before it begins if biblical Trinitarian categories establish the framework of the issue.

Another example where the decision to avoid Trinitarian language and categories has handicapped and hurt Stone-Campbell churches is in the area of the Holy Spirit. In certain sectors of the church of Christ, the Holy Spirit is relegated to a mere ancillary role of delivering the New Testament. There is even a strain of Holy Spirit deism which denies the real, personal indwelling of the Holy Spirit in the Christian.[11] The nip/tuck relationship between Stone-Campbell churches, even churches of Christ in particular, is due in large part to the deliberate avoidance of Trinitarian language. The strained relationship between the Holy Spirit and members of the church of Christ is rooted in the historic rejection of categories pertaining to the doctrine of the Trinity in particular.

RECLAIMING THE TRINITY

Typically, our approach to the gospel has often been anthropocentric (human-centered). Often the gospel begins with us, humans. It is focused on our need or on what we do. For example, since *we* needed salvation, God acted. However, long before we existed, and therefore, long before we had a need for salvation, God existed and had determined to glorify himself. In addition, in order to obtain salvation, we must hear, believe, repent, confess, and be baptized; we must obey the gospel. However, long before we even had the opportunity to do anything, God was at work, active in eternity and from eternity. So prior to our need and prior to our actions of obedience, God's action and work comes first. When it comes to the gospel, God must take priority. Indeed, the gospel begins with God, even the triune God.

The doctrine of the Trinity has bearing upon all aspects of the gospel. For example, Bruce A. Ware, in his chapter "Christ's Atonement" which he contributed to *Jesus in Trinitarian Perspective*, situates the atonement within a Trinitarian perspective. He frames his chapter around the question, "Why must God be three in one for salvation to be effected?"[12] Ware argues at length that the Son was chosen and sent by the Father from eternity to accomplish pardon from sin for humans. The Son in turn voluntarily empties himself so that he can come into the world and do the Father's will. He

---

11. Taylor, *Holy Spirit*, 111–15, makes this case adamantly that the Holy Spirit does not "actually, bodily, literally, personally, and directly" indwell believers (see esp. 111, 114).

12. Ware, "Christ's Atonement," 158.

then lives by the Spirit so that he can offer "unceasing, free obedience" to his Father.[13] The Son's Spirit-aided obedience culminates in death on the cross in order that the Father's just judgment could be satisfied and human sin atoned for in Christ. So the Son obeys the Father by the Spirit, an ordering of the life of the Trinity (*taxis*) issuing from eternity and revealed in the reality of atonement wrought in Christ.

The purpose of this book is to further explore the impact our doctrine of the Trinity has upon the gospel. The intention is to explore the priority of the triune God in the gospel. The aim is to ponder the great work of the Father, the Son, and the Holy Spirit in the salvation of God's people. Finally, to demonstrate the single divine intention of the triune God in the gospel is the glorification of the triune God in the redemption of a people. In this way, we will see "the light of the gospel of the glory of Christ, who is the image of God." Why? "For God, who said, 'Let light shine out of darkness,' has shone in our hearts to give the light of the knowledge of the glory of God in the face of Jesus Christ" (2 Cor 4:4, 6).

First, we turn our attention to the reality of the single, harmonious divine intention within the Trinity toward redemption which is at the heart of the gospel.

---

13. Ware, "Christ's Atonement," 175.

Chapter 2

A Single and Harmonious Divine Intention

No one person of the Godhead operates independently of the other two. That is, the Father does not act unilaterally or in opposition to the Son and the Spirit, nor the Son independent of the Father and the Spirit, nor the Spirit in opposition to the Father and the Son. All three persons of the Godhead—the Father, the Son, and the Holy Spirit—operate according to a single, harmonious intention. Their work is one, and they agree in this work. This single, harmonious divine intention is demonstrable from the biblical text, especially from the gospel of John.

THE HARMONY BETWEEN THE FATHER AND THE SON

The harmony which exists between God the Father and God the Son is seen in Jesus' statements concerning what he speaks and what he does being only that which the Father wills for him to speak and do. Jesus never spoke or acted in a way which was opposed to or different than what the Father intended. Jesus said and did what the Father desired him to say and do.

During his earthly ministry, Jesus said several times how his will and the Father's will are united. It is because the Father loves the Son that he "has given all things into [the Son's] hands" (John 3:35). What the Father has, the Son has also. The unity within the Godhead is seen in that "whatever the Father does, that the Son does likewise" (5:19). Jesus says, "I have come down from heaven, not to do My own will but the will of him who sent Me" (John 6:38). The Son always does what is pleasing to the Father (8:29). The very words Christ spoke are "as the Father has told Me" (12:50). Such perfect obedience and revelation by the Son is exactly what the Father desires and accords with the intention of the Godhead. So the Son's will and the Father's will are harmonious with a single intention.

The reason for such unity within the wills of the Father and the Son is that, as Jesus says, "I am in the Father and the Father is in Me" (John 14:10). "The Father is in Me and I am in the Father" (10:38; cf. 17:21). These are statements which were marshalled in the development of the doctrine of perichoresis—the interpenetration within the Godhead wherein the Father is in the Son, the Son is in the Father, the Father and the Son are in the Holy Spirit, and the Holy Spirit is in the Father and the Son. Such mutual indwelling further accentuates the harmonious union of intention and purpose in the work and words of redemption.

THE HARMONY BETWEEN THE FATHER, THE SON, AND THE HOLY SPIRIT

Since two persons of the Godhead are in accord in their intentions, it is not surprising to find that the third person of the Godhead is similarly in accord with them. Few statements better demonstrate the harmony between the Father, the Son, and the Holy Spirit than John 16:13–15:

> When the Spirit of truth comes, he will guide you into all the truth, for he will not speak on his own authority, but whatever he hears he will speak, and he will declare to you the things that are to come. He will glorify me, for he will take what is mine and declare it to you. All that the Father has is mine; therefore I said that he will take what is mine and declare it to you (John 16:13–15).

As part of his final discourse to his disciple on the night he is betrayed, Jesus promises to send another helper, the Holy Spirit, to be with his disciples forever (John 14:16). In addition, in promising the Holy Spirit to his disciples, Jesus said, "He will not speak on His own authority, but whatever He hears He will speak" (John 16:13).

Rendered in a literal manner, Jesus says the Holy Spirit "will not speak from Himself" (*aph heautou*). This is remarkably similar to Jesus' statement

A Single and Harmonious Divine Intention

"I do nothing from Myself" (8:28, *aph emautou*). To act or speak "from Himself" would mean that the Son or the Holy Spirit would act or speak without reference to the other members of the Godhead. Rather, both the Son and the Spirit act in concert with the divine intention. Thus, the Son speaks "just as the Father taught Me" (8:28b). Likewise, the Spirit speaks "whatever He hears" from the Father and the Son.

Such behavior, far from subordinating one or more persons of the Godhead to other members, is aimed at the divine end of mutual glorification. So Jesus says, "He will glorify Me" (16:14). That is, the Holy Spirit will glorify the Son. Similarly, the Son would be glorified by the Father in the Father's presence (17:5; cf. 13:31). Further, the Son glorified the Father while on earth (17:4; cf. 13:31). So the Father glorifies the Son; the Son glorifies the Father; the Holy Spirit glorifies the Son, which is also to glorify the Father. Therefore, the single, harmonious intention of the Trinity is aimed at a single divine end: mutual glorification within the Trinity.

But the Trinitarian knot is tightened when Jesus further explains the Holy Spirit "will take what is mine and declare it to you. All that the Father has is mine; therefore I said that he will take what is mine and declare it to you" (16:14b-15). First, the Spirit takes what is the Son's for the purpose of revealing it to the apostles. The Son does not horde or keep anything from the Spirit. The Son freely gives to the Spirit. He in turn gives it to the apostles. In this, the Spirit glorifies the Son. Second, all that belongs to the Father also belongs to the Son. Again, there is no selfish hoarding by the Father, keeping anything from the Son. Rather, the Father is pleased to share with the Son all that is his. Further, the Father and the Son are likewise pleased to share all that is theirs with the Spirit. Since they share all things, we catch a glimpse of the harmony within the Trinity. Nothing is hidden or held back. All things are shared, including the work and words of redemption. There is perfect agreement and accord within the Trinity so that each person of the Godhead can look upon all things and say, "Mine."

At the same time, within the unity that exists among the Godhead there is also distinction and differentiation. While the Son has "many things to say" to his disciples, they could not bear them at that time (16:12). Therefore, the Father and the Son would send the Holy Spirit. It would be the Holy Spirit, not the Son, who would guide the disciples into all truth (16:13b). Yet, while certainly "another Helper" (14:16), the Holy Spirit is taking what is the Father's and the Son's (viz., truth) and making that known to the disciples. Distinction of persons with unity of intention.

A Single and Harmonious Divine Intention

There is no disharmony or discord amongst the Trinity. It is not that the Father is doing one thing, but then the Son is doing another thing which is different than what the Father is doing, and then the Holy Spirit does yet a third thing which is completely different than what the Father and the Son were doing. The Spirit's will is in harmonious agreement with the will of the Father and the Son. So we do not have three disharmonious wills in opposition or disagreement. Rather, we have a single divine intention pursued fully by the Father, and the Son, and the Holy Spirit.

The work of the Trinity is a single, harmonious work, whether that is the work of creation or the work of new creation. Therefore, while the Son is the one given *by* the Father (conceived by the Holy Spirit) for saving sinners, the Holy Spirit is the one given *to* the redeemed, having been sent by the Father and the Son. The love, grace, and wisdom of the whole Godhead is manifest in the Father sending his Son to be incarnate and suffer for sinners, and in the Father and the Son sending the Holy Spirit to apply the completed work of Calvary to sinners.

A VOICE FROM THE PAST

While the concept of a single harmonious divine intention without confusion of the distinct persons of the Godhead may be new territory for certain readers, there is precedent within the Restoration Movement for just such biblical teaching. Having established the case on biblical grounds, appeal can be made to none other than Alexander Campbell during his debate with Nathan Lewis Rice on the influence of the Holy Spirit in conversion:

> The revelation of Father, Son and Holy Spirit is not more clear and distinct than are the different offices assumed and performed by these glorious and ineffable Three in the present affairs of the universe. It is true, so far as unity of design and concurrence of action are contemplated, they co-operate in every work of creation, providence and redemption. Such is the concurrence expressed by the Messiah in these words—"My Father worketh hitherto, and I work"—"I and my Father are one"—"Whatsoever the Father doeth, the Son doeth likewise:" but not such a concurrence as annuls personality, impairs or interferes with the distinct offices of each in the salvation of man. For example: the Father sends his Son, and not the Son his Father. The Father provides a body and a soul for his Son, and not the Son for his Father. The Son offers up that body and soul for sin, and thus expiates it, which the Father does not,

A Single and Harmonious Divine Intention

> but accepts it. The Father and the Son send forth the Spirit, and not the Spirit either. The Spirit now advocates Christ's cause, and not Christ his own cause. The Holy Spirit now animates the church with his presence, and not Christ himself. He is the Head of the church, while the Spirit is the heart of it. The Father originates all, the Son executes alt [sic], the Spirit consummates all. Eternal volition, design and mission belong to the Father; reconciliation to the Son; sanctification to the Spirit. In each of these terms there are numerous terms and ideas of subordinate extent, to which we cannot now advert.[1]

Campbell here makes the distinction within the Godhead of the diverse, though inseparable, operations of the various persons of the Trinity. The Father sends the Son, not the Son the Father; The Son dies for sin, not the Father, though the Father accepts it; The Spirit is sent by the Father and the Son, not vice versa. The Father is the originator, the Son the executor, and the Spirit the consummator. It is my aim in this study to explore the "numerous terms and ideas of subordinate extent" that are related to the work of the triune God in accomplishing the singular divine intention behind human redemption.

DISTINCT-BUT-INSEPARABLE ROLES IN THE TRINITY

The classic formulations are that where the Son is, there is the Father and the Spirit; where the Spirit is, there is the Father and the Son; where the Father is, there is the Son and the Spirit.[2] At the same time, each person of the Godhead has a distinct role in the redemption of humans. Thus, it is the Father who elects, not the Son or the Spirit, though it is in Christ and according to the Spirit. It is the Son who dies on the cross, not the Father nor the Spirit, though he offers himself through the Spirit to the Father. It is the Spirit who applies the completed work, not the Father nor the Son, though it is in the Son and according to the purpose of the Father. So while each person of the Godhead has a distinct role in redemption, they never operate independent of one another.

Scripture reveals that it is the Father who takes the lead in redemption predestined through election in Christ (Eph 1:4). Scripture also shows that it is the Son who accomplished redemption on the cross, having been sent

---

1. Gould, *Debate*, 616.

2. One example of this is Ambrose in his work "On the Holy Spirit:" "for where the Paraclete Spirit is, there is also the Son" (Ambrose of Milan, "Three Books," 111).

by the Father (Gal 4:4–5). Scripture also demonstrates how the Spirit is the primary agent in applying the completed work of Christ to the children of God (Gal 4:6). Yet, "when one person of the Trinity acts, the others are not somehow absent or passive or mere spectators."[3] The entire Trinity is active in redemption from eternity to eternity: from predestination, to accomplishment, to application, to glorification. At the same time, in everything, the three persons of the Trinity act in harmonious accord. No one person acts without all having a part. This is the harmony which exists within the Trinity in redemption.

THE TRIUNE GOD IN REDEMPTION

Few passages of Scripture bring this truth to the fore as 1 Pet 1:1–2. In the opening lines of his first epistle, Peter addresses his audience with a profound and foundational truth: the sanctifying work of the triune God in the lives of believers. This truth, though succinctly stated, carries within it profound implications for the understanding of God's nature and his redemptive plan for humanity:

> Peter, an apostle of Jesus Christ, To those who are elect exiles of the Dispersion in Pontus, Galatia, Cappadocia, Asia, and Bithynia, according to the foreknowledge of God the Father, in the sanctification of the Spirit, for obedience to Jesus Christ and for sprinkling with his blood: May grace and peace be multiplied to you. (1 Pet 1:1–2)

Immediately evident is that this passage is Trinitarian. God the Father, God the Son, and God the Holy Spirit are all mentioned, though not in that order. The Father foreknew the elect exiles, the Son sprinkles them with his blood, and the Spirit sanctifies them. This triadic expression of God's work reveals the foundational truth of the Christian faith: that God is triune, existing eternally as Father, Son, and Holy Spirit. Moreover, all three persons of the Trinity are at work on behalf of the "elect exiles of the Dispersion in Pontus," etc. There is not a hint of division or confusion in the actions taken by the Trinity. The work of the Father, the Son, and the Holy Spirit is not independent of one another but is harmoniously coordinated towards the same redemptive end. While each person has their respective work, they all operate in harmony with one another.

3. Gibson, "Glorious, Indivisible, Trinitarian Work of God in Christ," 364.

A Single and Harmonious Divine Intention

First, "foreknowledge" belongs to the Father. Often the case is made that foreknowledge simply means "know in advance." According to this view, foreknowledge is reduced to mere prescience. Acts 26:5 and 2 Pet 3:17 are cited as examples. However, in these texts humans are the subject of the verb (*proginōskō*, used participially). Such "knowing beforehand" is vastly different from God's foreknowledge. Wayne Grudem suggests that the whole phrase "elect exiles of the Dispersion in Pontus, Galatia, etc." is what is "according to the foreknowledge of God the Father." So "their status as sojourners, their privileges as God's chosen people, even their hostile environment in [Asia Minor], were all known by God before the world began, all came about in accordance with his foreknowledge, and thus (we may conclude) all were in accordance with his fatherly love for his own people."[4] It is the elect who are the objects of divine foreknowledge. The Father foreknew his elect. He foreknew everything about them, including their election unto salvation.

A key verse for keeping a proper perspective on divine foreknowledge is a few verses later in 1 Pet 1:20, which says, "[Christ] was foreknown before the foundation of the world but was made manifest in the last times for the sake of you." Commenting on Christ being "foreknown," Thomas Schriener writes, "Peter was not merely saying that God foresaw when Christ would come, though that is part of his meaning. He was also saying that God foreordained when Christ would come. Indeed, God had to plan when he would come since Christ was sent by God. Christ's coming hardly depends on human choices."[5]

Similarly, divine sovereignty and initiation in the salvation of God's elect are accentuated in 1 Pet 1:2. Before creation, God the Father, in agreement with the Son and the Spirit, set his love upon these sinners in Asia Minor and chose them for the grace of sprinkling with Christ's blood and the glory of sanctification by the Spirit. The Father lovingly ordered things so that these elect exiles would live where they live, hear the gospel, and obey Christ. The Father's foreknowledge is the root and foundation of election.

Second, sanctification belongs to the Holy Spirit "in sanctification of the Spirit" or "by the sanctification of the Spirit." Once more these elect exiles are the objects of the sanctification of the Spirit. They are elect exiles by means of the sanctifying work of the Holy Spirit. That is, the Holy Spirit set these peoples of Asia Minor apart as God's chosen people. While

---

4. Grudem, *1 Peter*, 50.
5. Schreiner, *1, 2 Peter, Jude*, 53–54.

A Single and Harmonious Divine Intention

divine foreknowledge reaches into eternity past, the work of the Spirit in sanctifying the elect occurs in due time. In due time, and in agreement with the Father and the Son, the Spirit makes the elect holy unto God (cf. 2 Thess 2:13). Sanctification or to be set apart was always for a purpose, viz., service. The Holy Spirit both sets Christians apart for service and enables them to perform that service.

If the Father's foreknowledge points readers to eternity past, the Spirit's work of sanctification points to the Christian's present reality. The Spirit is setting apart elect exiles more and more to look like Christ in holiness, faith, and conduct. The Spirit's work is also in agreement with the Father's work from eternity. Those foreknown by the Father before time are the same ones who are sanctified by the Spirit in time.

Finally, obedience and sprinkling belong to the Son, Jesus Christ. "For obedience to Jesus Christ and for sprinkling with His blood." If foreknowledge is the work of the Father in the past, and the sanctification of the Spirit is the present work of the Spirit, it may be that obedience and sprinkling looks forward to the future. The Son, in agreement with the Father and the Spirit, continually sprinkles his blood upon these elect exiles for the forgiveness of their sins.

The Christian's life ought to be leading toward more and more obedience to Christ. Daily our obedience to Lord Jesus should increase. But it is also the Christian's imperfect experience which reminds that obedience is often incomplete. The blood of Jesus Christ is necessary to sprinkle our afflicted and guilty conscience. Thus, the faithful Christian life is marked by obedience whose failings are cleansed by the blood of Christ. It is daily continual obedience and forgiveness. Those foreknown by the Father and sanctified by the Spirit are those who are sprinkled by the blood of the Son and obey him.

Peter seamlessly weaves the Trinity into the introduction of his epistle. He also points to their respective work in election, sanctification, and salvation. It must be stressed that this is not three works done separately, perhaps even disharmoniously, by each of the three persons of the Godhead. Rather, it is a single work done in harmonious concert by all three persons of the Trinity. The Father's election, the Son's atonement, and the Spirit's sanctification are all part of a unified and seamless work of redemption that reflects the perfect unity and harmony of the triune God. The Father, the Son, and the Holy Spirit are in perfect agreement in their work of saving people.

Part I

Redemption Predestined

THE GOSPEL BEGINS WITH God. Specifically, it begins with the triune God in eternity. The work of the Trinity in salvation begins before the beginning. A key phrase found in the Bible which has bearing upon the work of God in eternity is "before the foundation of the world." The phrase assumes there was a beginning, a moment when the world was founded. Further, it assumes there was existence prior to the moment of time when creation leapt into existence. Typically, this existence prior to creation is denoted as "eternity past," i.e., the existence God enjoyed in eternity prior to his work in creation.

Several Bible verses describe how in eternity the Father, the Son, and the Holy Spirit existed with one another in glorious union. It is in this eternal existence when the Father, the Son, and the Holy Spirit, according to their kingly freedom (i.e., sovereignty), are active: foreknowing, foreordaining, predetermining, predestining, choosing, decreeing—all according to their kingly freedom (sovereignty).

Before the foundation of the world, the Father, Son, and Holy Spirit exist in a relationship of love and glory (John 17:5, 24). Before the foundation of the world, God chose people in Christ and in love predestined them to adoption to himself as sons through Jesus Christ (Eph 1:4–5). Before the ages began, God the Father gave his gracious purpose of salvation and sanctification to people in Christ (2 Tim 1:9). Before the ages began, God promised himself to grant faith, truth, and hope of eternal life to his elect (Titus 1:2). Given the foregoing, it is reasonable to conclude that before the

Part I: Redemption Predestined

foundation of the world, God wrote names in the Lamb's book of life (cf. Rev 13:8; 17:8).

Admittedly, these are deep waters. There is depth in exploring the eternal workings of the triune God. As Lenski points out, "Any *eternal* act of God's pertaining to 'us' in *time* is bound to offer difficulty to our minds and our thinking."[1] The infinite triune God cannot fit into our finite minds. There is mystery involved with the Trinity, especially pertaining to the question of what the triune God was doing prior to the creation of the world. Yet, there are glimpses past the veil of eternity which can be explored to a certain extent. The following chapters explore the several places where the phrases "before the world existed," "before the foundation of the world," and "before time began" are found. Special attention will be given to the work of the triune God described in those various contexts.

---

1. Lenski, *Galatians, Ephesians, and Philippians*, 357. Emphasis original.

Chapter 3

The Glorification of a People Given by the Father to the Son from Eternity

John 17 is a high point not only in John's gospel but the entire Bible. It is commonly called Jesus' high priestly prayer, wherein he prays to the Father for his people. What is sometimes missed is that this is inter-Trinitarian communication: the Son is talking to the Father, the Spirit interceding on behalf of Jesus the Man. The preexistence and deity of the Son are evident.

More than that, the actions of the Trinity "before the world existed" are revealed. Think about it: "What is God doing when God is not doing anything in the world because God has yet to create the world?" One may be tempted to say that God is doing nothing, but such a conclusion fails to recognize the depth of Jesus' prayer in John 17. In fact, the Father, the Son, and the Holy Spirit are relationally active in inter-Trinitarian self-glorifying love:

> And now, Father, glorify me in your own presence with the glory that I had with you before the world existed. (John 17:5)

The existence of the Godhead prior to the existence of the world is clear. The Father and the Son existed in eternity with one another (cf. John 1:1, "the Word was *with* God"). Also, the mutual Trinitarian glory possessed by the Father and the Son (and the Holy Spirit too no doubt, though the Spirit is not specifically mentioned) is seen. First, the Son petitions the Father "glorify Me together with Yourself" (NASB), or lit. "from Yourself" (*para seautō*). At the same time, this is glory which the Son "had" or possessed "before the world existed." The use of the imperfect tense further accentuates that it was always his possession from eternity. The Son existed in glory with the Father "before the world existed." With the incarnation came a veiling of that glory so that he could take on human nature. Nevertheless, it is the Son's own glory with the Father which he prays to be glorified with by the Father. So the text points us to the glorious eternal existence ("before the world existed") of Father, Son, and Holy Spirit.

Second, the mutual glorifying relationship which exists between the Trinity from eternity is also evident in this petition of Jesus. Jesus asks the Father to "glorify Me." Elsewhere in John, Jesus has affirmed more than once that he has glorified the Father, especially in his death (13:31–32; 14:13). In addition, during his ministry, the Father glorified the Son (John 8:54; cf. 11:4). Indeed, in the previous verse Jesus declares, "I glorified you on the earth" (17:4). The prayer began with the petition, "Glorify the Son that the Son may glorify You" (v.1). Thus, there is a relationship of mutual glorification which exists within the triune God. This mutually glorifying relationship existed "before the world existed." So from eternity, the Trinity has existed in a mutually glorifying relationship. The Father glorifies the Son; the Son glorifies the Father; the Spirit glorifies the Father and the Son.[1]

The mutual glorification of the Godhead by the three persons who comprise the Godhead is vital to understanding the whole aim and goal of the work of the triune God. At the heart of their work—election, atonement, sanctification, and glorification—is the triune God's intention of glorifying one another, i.e., the Father glorifying the Son and the Spirit; the Son glorifying the Father and the Spirit; the Spirit glorifying the Father and the Son. Everything the Father, the Son, and the Holy Spirit do before time, in time, and at the end of time, from eternity to eternity is aimed at glorifying one another.

It is the mutual Trinitarian glory which Jesus has in mind when he prays for his people, "Those who will believe in Me through their word," i.e., those given to him by the Father. The Son prays to the Father on their behalf:

> Father, I desire that they also, whom you have given me, may be with me where I am, to see my glory that you have given me because you loved me before the foundation of the world. (John 17:24)

---

1. The Spirit's glorification of the Father and the Son was demonstrated when John 16:13–15 was examined in the previous chapter.

The Glorification of a People Given by the Father to the Son from Eternity

Yet again the existence of the Godhead "before the foundation of the world" is clear. Here, an added emphasis of mutual love between the Father and the Son is presented. "You loved Me," the Son says to the Father. That inter-Trinitarian love within the Godhead was reality "before the foundation of the world." This is the love of the Father for the Son from eternity.

Indeed, "before the foundation of the world" is the timestamp for this verse. The Father's love of the Son is from eternity. So also is the glory given to the Son by the Father. The perfect tense ("You have given") indicates that the Son's glory was given him by the Father in love "before the foundation of the world," and he continues to possess his own glory. It is this glory which Christ desires/wills for those whom the Father has given him to see or experience. We must not miss the parallel: even as the Father gave the Son glory from eternity which he continues to possess, so also the Father has given people—as a unit (*ho*, "that which You have given Me") and individually (*kakeinoi*, "also those," or "they also")—to the Son from eternity which he continues to possess. Both the giving of glory and people to the Son occur "before the foundation of the world." The verbs agree in all aspects; indeed, the same word is used for "given" (*dedōkas*), both in reference to the glory given by the Father to the Son and those given by the Father to the Son. Therefore, "before the foundation of the world" the Father loved the Son, the Father gave glory to the Son, and the Father gave people—both as a unit and individually—to the Son.

Further, it is the will ("I desire," *thelō*) of the Son that those given to him by the Father "be with Me where I am" (NASB). So the Father gives people to the Son from eternity whom the Son wills be with him and experience his glory in eternity. One must also keep in mind that the will of the Son is also the will of the Father (cf. John 5:30; 6:38). Further, it has already been established that there is a single, harmonious divine intention within the Trinity (see chapter 2). Therefore, just as the Son wills that those given to him by the Father see his glory, it is likewise the will of the Father and the Spirit that these same ones see the Son's glory. Are we to assume that the Son's will can be frustrated? Can the will of the triune God from eternity be thwarted? Such questions are answered in the negative when it is remembered that the whole work of the Trinity toward people is rooted in the inter-Trinitarian, self-glorifying love of the Father, the Son, and the Holy Spirit from before all time.

It must not be overlooked that there is a parallel between the Father giving glory to the Son because the Father loves the Son and the Father

Part I: Redemption Predestined

giving a specific people to the Son because the Father loved them even as he loved the Son (vs. 23b–24). Given this parallel, the timestamp for the Father's love of the Son and the Father's love of the people he gives to the Son would be identical: "before the foundation of the world." The love the Father has for the Son is specific and personal. There is no reason contextually why the love the Father has for those he gives the Son should be any less specific or personal. Indeed, the love the Father has for those he gives to the Son is the same ("even as") as the Father's love for the Son.[2]

Those who are loved by the Father and given by the Father to the Son are "the ones believing in Me" through the apostolic word (v. 20). Hence, the incarnate Son is praying for future believers who "before the foundation of the world" were given in love by the Father to him. The time-bending aspect of this is truly remarkable, and our finite minds struggle to understand it. Suffice it to say that "before the foundation of the world" from the whole fallen mass of humanity, the Father set his affection on a specific people based solely on his good intention and grace. Those whom the Father loved he gave to the Son whom he loved from eternity. The incarnate Son prays for all those given him by the Father, including those future believers (who at the time of the prayer have yet to be born and therefore are yet to believe). The Son then goes to the cross to die in the place of all those who are given to him by the Father in order that they be with the Son and see his glory in eternity, glory which the Father gave him from eternity.

There is an unbroken chain from eternity to eternity present in the prayer of Jesus. The Father loved a particular people whom he gave to the Son before the foundation of the world (cf. Heb 2:13b). The Son, in time, prays for these and then dies on their behalf for their sins. These same ones are preserved and brought to glory at the end of time that they may see the Son's glory. Indeed, his glory is their glory (John 17:22). The Father's love for the Son is the same love for them (v. 23). The Son's place is their place (v. 24). In this prayer Jesus affirms that he and all those given to him by his Father will dwell together in eternity.

---

2. It is the same word in all three places: *ēgapēsas*. "so that the world may know that You . . . loved them even as You loved Me . . . You loved Me before the foundation of the world" (vs. 23b, 24).

Chapter 4

The Choice of a People by the Father in the Son from Eternity

Ephesians is written by the apostle Paul to saints, Christians. He opens his epistle praising God the Father as the one "who blessed us in Christ with every spiritual blessing in the heavenly places." The Father is "the One blessing" with "every spiritual blessing." The Father blesses "us," i.e., saints, Christians, the faithful in Christ Jesus (v. 2). This is a specific people, distinct from the world, non-Christians, unbelievers who are "separated from Christ" (2:12). The Father has blessed us . . .

> even as he chose us in him before the foundation of the world, that we should be holy and blameless before him. In love he predestined us for adoption to himself as sons through Jesus Christ, according to the purpose of his will. (Eph 1:4–5)

"Just as" (NASB) the Father has blessed those in Christ, so too "He [the Father] chose us [saints, Christians, the faithful] in Him [the Son]." Based on his kingly freedom (sovereignty) and "according to the purpose of His will" (v. 5b), the Father chose his people.

The temptation is to center the time of this choice in time, space, and history and the locus of the choice in humans. Indeed, Avon Malone writes, "Man, made in God's image, has the crucial power to choose."[1] So for

---

1. Malone, *Purpose and the People*, 16.

Part I: Redemption Predestined

Malone what it means to be made in God's image is the power to choose. The assumption is that the Bible teaches that the divine image in humans is the free will. However, this is nowhere taught. Even if it were, due to sin the divine image is marred, broken, in need of restoration. Hence, it follows that if the divine image is freedom of the will, due to sin it must be in bondage to sin or, at best, grossly faulty and unable to operate at optimal levels. At best, this would leave humans at a severe disadvantage when it came to choosing Christ, assuming they were able to at all. Malone goes on to mention "the Bible's emphasis on free will."[2] Where does the Bible teach the doctrine of free will? Everywhere is taught the freedom of God. God's will is never thwarted (Job 42:2); "the counsel of Yahweh stands forever" (Ps 33:11). However, human will is often thwarted (1 Cor 1:19), our counsel and plans come to nothing and are frustrated (Ps 33:10). Thus, the autonomous free will of humans is merely an assumption with no biblical foundation. So the locus of choice must be found elsewhere and the time element is further displaced from time-bound humans.

The Holy Spirit through Paul identifies the locus of the choice: the Father. God the Father is the subject of the verb "chose." Thus, "He chose" means the Father chose. The object of the verb is "us." This would include Paul (1:1), Tychicus (6:21), and all the saints to whom Paul is writing. In short, "us" is the Christians to whom Paul wrote, Paul and Tychicus included. This is a specific people, even God's people. Thus, "He chose us" means God the Father chose a specific people, even his own people.

Once more, the temptation is to minimize the force of the text. Malone writes, "God *envisioned* a people in Christ."[3] First, the text says no such thing. The text says God chose. Second, this reading is based on a faulty understanding of foreknowledge as merely "pre-vision."[4] Such a passive view of foreknowledge envisions God looking down the corridors of time to see the free will actions of humans and then making his choice based upon the choices of humans. Such an understanding of foreknowledge is not how Scripture presents God foreknowing. God actively foreknows. In addition, Paul is emphatic that God's choice is first.

God's choice of his people is an act of divine mercy and love. It is not arbitrary since it is "according to the purpose of His will" (v. 5) and is part of "the counsel of His will" (v. 11). Infinite intelligence, perfect wisdom,

---

2. Malone, *Purpose and the People*, 16.
3. Malone, *Purpose and the People*, 17. Emphasis added.
4. Malone, *Purpose and the People*, 17.

The Choice of a People by the Father in the Son from Eternity

and unfathomable knowledge is involved with the purpose and counsel of the will of the triune God. Further insight into the choice of God is seen when Scripture says God did not choose Israel because of anything in them, whether it be their number (Deut 7:6–8), their righteousness, or how upright their heart is (9:5–6). God chose his people "because Yahweh loves you" and to keep his own word (7:8; 9:6). So also the election of the saved occurs "not because of works done by us in righteousness" (Titus 3:5); it is an act of his great steadfast love, mercy, and grace that he has chosen his people as a heritage. It is for his own sake and according to the purpose and counsel of his will that "He chose us."

God the Father chose a specific people "in Him," i.e., in Christ. So the Father chose us in Christ. Everything about election here is personal: it is not a plan nor a process. The Father chooses "us"—every single Christian to whom the letter is written, including Paul, an apostle according to God's will (v. 1)—in Christ. Just as the Trinity is personal, so the choice of an elect people is personal.

Many have attempted to extricate the personal aspect of election from this verse. Within the Restoration Movement, Glen Osburn, writing for a church of Christ commentary, writes, "Because of God's character, this choice was not of particular individuals but of the essentials in the plan of salvation."[5] The text itself militates against this statement. "Us" is a personal pronoun, and it is the object of God's action. Osburn's statement is even more quixotic since just prior to this he wrote, "Before we could choose him, He chose us."[6] This is accurate to the text and likewise militates against Osburn's own interpretation of the choice not being personal but impersonal (i.e., of a plan). Sanders identifies the shortcoming of other possibilities:

> The other possible answers are either unworthily weak (we were present in the mind of God with an ideal rather than actual preexistence, which, by the way, would be all that the Son of God shares: a merely ideal preexistence), or require some sort of coeternal preexistence of all creation (everything is actually there with God in eternity past, and merely manifests itself in the course of history).[7]

No amount of explaining can eliminate the personal aspect of election. God's choice is personal. "He chose us."

5. Osburn, "Ephesians."
6. Osburn, "Ephesians."
7. Sanders, *Triune God*, 207.

Part I: Redemption Predestined

Then, there is the timestamp: "before the foundation of the world." As John Eadie writes, "The phrase itself declares that this election is no act of time, for time dates from the creation. Prior to the commencement of time were we chosen in Christ."[8] When did the Father choose "us" in Christ? Paul gives the timestamp for when this occurred: in eternity past prior to the beginning of time. Before all time, in eternity. So the divine action of the Father in Christ in the election of people took place "before" the world was created.

One translational and interpretive challenge is determining if "in love" belongs with the preceding or the forthcoming. In other words, does "in love" describe God's work in electing a particular people, or does it describe his work in predestining those whom he chose for adoption? It is fitting that the phrase is sandwiched between both of these substantial doctrines because whether it describes one or the other, the work of the triune God in both election and predestination is a work done "in love." God's eternal love is the basis of his electing and predestining people. John Murray writes, "The love of God from which the atonement springs is not a distinctionless love; it is a love that elects and predestines."[9] Such a consideration ought to wave people off of thinking that these doctrines are somehow monstrous or bad.

Related to election is predestination. Hence, verse 5 begins, "He predestined us for adoption to Himself as sons through Jesus Christ." Every Bible believing Christian believes in predestination if for no other reason than the word is in their Bible. The question is not whether or not the Bible teaches predestination; the question is, "What does the Bible teach about predestination?" As to the word "predestined,"[10] the lexical data is virtually univocal that it means to decide or determine beforehand, pre-ordain or foreordain, and predestine. BDAG is typical with "**predetermine**, of God."[11] What is it that God has predestined?

As with election, once more "predestined" is the action of God the Father; he is the subject of the participle.[12] Once more, like the main verb, the

---

8. Eadie, *Commentary on the Greek Text*, 20–21.
9. Murray, *Redemption Accomplished and Applied*, 4.
10. Gk. *proorisas*.
11. BDAG, 873. Emphasis original.
12. Grammatically, *proorisas* is a participle related to the main verb in verse 4, *exelexato*. Hence, grammatically, election and predestination are related, and being the same tense strengthens the case for the contemporaneous nature of these actions.

The Choice of a People by the Father in the Son from Eternity

object of the participle is "us," i.e., Christians. God predestines people for "adoption through Jesus Christ." In fact, the same people are the recipients of the divine action in both verses, viz., us.

We may ask, "When did the predestination take place?" The time-stamp remains the same: from eternity, before creation. Indeed, both the main verb and the participle are aorist tense, making these actions of God contemporaneous.[13] Hence, election and predestination are actions taken by God, even the Father, "before the foundation of the world."

The action of the Father in eternity is seen in relation to the work of the Son in time. Therefore, God predestines people "to adoption as sons through Jesus Christ to Himself" (LSB). *Adoption* is a family term. The church is the Family of God. The Father chose us and adopted us into his family. We are transferred from the dysfunctional family of Satan to the glorious family of God; we are sons and daughters of God with all the privileges that status bestows. What was predestined "before the foundation of the world" is realized in history as all those chosen by the Father in Christ are ushered into God's family through Christ in due time. Christ, through his atoning work, makes adoption a reality. All those chosen in the Son in eternity are then made sons of God by adoption in time.

Unfortunately, the exegesis of Eph 1:4–5 offered above has not found a favorable reception in the Restoration Movement. Burton Coffman's commentaries on the Bible have a wide reading in churches of Christ. Coffman wrote the following on the word "predestined":

> Much of the fog, as thick as the meringue on a pie, which has confused and obscured the meaning of Paul here, disappears in a little closer attention to the word "destined," the same being the principal part of the word "predestined," which is by far the favorite word of the scholars for this rendition. The syllable "pre" is simple enough and refers only to the time (before the foundation of the world) when God "destined" certain things to occur. Therefore, we shall let the time element rest for the moment and focus upon what is meant by "destined." God destined people to be conformed to the image of his Son, the meaning being obviously this that the destiny of every man ever born on earth was that he should obey God and be conformed to the image of God's Son. "Destined" has special reference to the plan of God, his intention, the objective he had in view when man was created.[14]

---

13. Lenski, *Galatians, Ephesians, and Philippians*, 360.
14. Coffman, "Commentary on Romans 8."

Part I: Redemption Predestined

When Rom 8:29–30 is covered in a later chapter, a closer examination of Coffman's universalization of predestination will be taken. Here, suffice to say that Coffman's linguistic gymnastics helps him avoid the personal nature of predestination. First, the atomization of the English word "predestine" into its constituent parts is unhelpful because it reads an English meaning into the Greek term. True, the prefix "pre-" means before, but "destined" is an English verb which Coffman confuses with destiny, an English noun. However, one does not determine the meaning of the original text by word studies in English (or any other language of translation).

Upon closer review of *proorizō* (the lemma), the prefix *pro-* can mean "before," but the phrase "before the foundation of the world" in the verse is the time reference which substantially pins down when God did his pre-destining work. However, *horizō*, the verbal root, is never translated close to what Coffman means by destiny. Depending upon context, it means appoint, determine, designate, or set limits (with other uses). Regardless, such reverse etymology only yields erroneous exegesis. Further, it avoids the normal usage of words within their given context.

The understanding of "predestined" produced by Coffman's reverse etymology simply does not fit with what Paul wrote. Coffman writes, "God 'destined' *certain things* to occur" (emphasis mine). He limits God's predestining work to "certain things." Not even all things. Moreover, the "certain things" God is said to predestine are further identified in the concluding sentence of the above quoted paragraph, viz., "*the plan of God*, his intention, the objective he has in view when man was created" (emphasis mine). Hence, the personal aspect of God's work in predestination (God "predestined *us*") is eliminated. Coffman would read Paul as writing that God "predestined a plan," not "He predestined us." No, it is not "certain things" which God predestines; it is a specific people including Paul and the faithful saints in Ephesus (v.1). It is actually Coffman's reading into the text which obscures Paul's meaning with "fog, as thick as meringue on a pie."

Another attempt to reinterpret predestination by Coffman is to pit the almighty will of humans against the sovereign free will of God. Coffman offers an example of an attempt to snatch the mighty will of humans from the sovereign will of God:

> But, if all people are thus "destined" by God to be Christians, why are not all saved? God gave every person the absolute freedom of his will, and any man can therefore accept or refuse the destiny to which God called him. A man can live against his destiny, as

evidenced by the fact that so many do; but, despite human sin, the essential glory of man's true destiny is undeniable.¹⁵

Coffman, like Malone above, must rescue human free will from God's predestining work. According to Coffman, humans have "the absolute freedom of his will" which enables them to "accept or refuse the destiny to which God called him." As demonstrated above, this de-personalizes predestination from people being the objects of God's determination to a mere plan. Worse, the proof of human free will is not a text of Scripture but experience: "A man can live against his destiny, *as evidenced by the fact that so many do*" (emphasis mine).

Contra Coffman, the solution to the issue of which will is ultimately sovereign is found in Eph 1. God's work in election and predestination both before time and in due time occurs "according to the good pleasure of his will" (LSB). The election and predestination of people is not according to their will. God's will is front and center in the work of redeeming people in Christ. Arnold points out that Paul could have written "God predestined us on the basis of [κατὰ] His will." The addition of "good pleasure" shows that the objection that God's choice is somehow arbitrary is misguided. Arnold writes, "The term 'good pleasure' (εὐδοκία), however, clarifies that God did not select a people in some austere, dispassionate way . . . God took great delight in thinking of his future people and being kindly disposed toward them."¹⁶ Therefore, election and predestination are based on God's will, and his will is good.

THE GIVING OF THE GRACIOUS PURPOSE BY THE FATHER TO A SPECIFIC PEOPLE IN ETERNITY

> Therefore do not be ashamed of the testimony about our Lord, nor of me his prisoner, but share in suffering for the gospel by the power of God, who saved us and called us to a holy calling, not because of our works but because of his own purpose and grace, which he gave us in Christ Jesus before the ages began, and which now has been manifested through the appearing of our Savior Christ Jesus, who abolished death and brought life and immortality to light through the gospel. (2 Tim 1:8–10)

---

15. Coffman, "Commentary on Romans 8."
16. Arnold, *Ephesians*, 83.

Part I: Redemption Predestined

As previously noted, the gospel begins with God, especially his "own purpose and grace, which he gave us in Christ Jesus before the ages began" (2 Tim 1:9). Before time began God purposed a purpose and then in time he worked "all things according to the counsel of His will" (Eph 1:11). Paul is emphatic that the gospel is theocentric, beginning and ending with God.

Next, there must be a recognition of sin and a need for a Savior who saves us from sin. "Our Lord" (2 Tim 1:8) is "our Savior Christ Jesus" (v. 10) who "saved us" (v. 9) from our sins. Our sins brought "death" (v. 10), both spiritual and physical death. Too many people view sin as a small thing, just finite deeds. Popular speakers like Rob Bell have unfortunately popularized such a diminished hamartiology. Bell writes about "finite sins . . . committed in the few years . . . spent on earth."[17] Rather, people must be convicted of their sins committed against a holy and eternal God. McRaney rightly notes, "All sin is sin against God, not just against insignificant people who will forget or get over it."[18] This same eternal God is the only one who, in the person of Jesus Christ, can erase all of our sins. The gospel "has been manifested through the appearing of our Savior Christ Jesus" (v. 10). In other words, God put on flesh, lived a sinless and perfect life among us, and died the death that was due us on the cross. In this way, he "brought life and immortality to light through the gospel" (v. 10b), that is, eternal life with God forever. God calls us through the gospel, and we respond with faith, repentance, and obedience.

God is "the one who saved us and called us," the participles agreeing in every aspect which would point to these potentially occurring contemporaneously (at the same time). When we are called by the gospel we are saved; we are saved when we are called. The calling is to holiness. Now that we are saved, we are to be holy according to that "holy calling." The holy God calls us to holy living.

We are saved "not because of our works." It was not because we were smart enough, or spiritual enough, or better than the one who is not saved. We are saved "because of His own purpose and grace." The contrast is sharp (*alla*): not works, *but* God's own purpose and grace. Or, taken as a hendiadys, because of God's own gracious purpose.[19] "Purpose" is often used in the NT in reference to God's purpose (Rom 8:28; 9:11; Eph 1:11; 3:11).

---

17. Bell, *Love Wins*, 102.
18. McRaney, *Art of Personal Evangelism*, 84.
19. "Which" (*tēn*) is a singular demonstrative and agrees with both "purpose" and "grace" in all aspects.

The Choice of a People by the Father in the Son from Eternity

Paul affirms that our salvation is not the result of anything we have done ("works"); our salvation is rooted squarely in the gracious purpose of God.

God's purpose cannot be earned since it is of "grace." Hence, "He [God] gave us" his gracious purpose "in Christ Jesus before the ages began [*pro chronōn aiōiōn*]." "Before the ages began" or "from all eternity" (NASB) is the timestamp for the giving of the Father's gracious purpose to a specific people in Christ Jesus. The Father giving his gracious purpose to his people in Christ Jesus took place in eternity before the beginning of time. God's grace and purpose is a gift "to us" in and from eternity. God's gracious purpose to save and call us is given to us before time began in eternity. The eternal gracious purpose of God the Father in Christ is the salvation and sanctification of a specific people.

As has been seen thus far, the salvation of specific people ("us") is rooted in God's gracious purpose (not human works) given to us before time began. However, Restoration Movement commentators once more aim to remove the personal aspect of this to an impersonal plan. Coffman writes of "the heavenly plan for man's salvation" and the application of this verse to "individuals as regards their personal salvation" is "a gross error."[20] Hill, writing for another Restoration Movement commentary, writes, "Paul tells Timothy this plan was put into place by God's wisdom long before Paul or Timothy ever declared it from their own lips, even before the world began."[21] Both commentators miss the force of Paul's words: it is not a "plan put into place;" it is God's own purpose and grace given to us. Further, if it is not a personal salvation, why does Paul say God "saved us"? Who is the "us" if not specific people including Paul himself? Once more the interpretation of Restoration Movement commentators does not do justice to what the text says.

Before the triune God founded the world, in love, the Father chose a specific people whom he gave to the Son. These same ones the Father also predestined for adoption into his family through the Son. Before time began, God gave his purpose and grace to all those whom he would save and call. These same ones will see the Son's glory when they are with him in glory.

---

20. Coffman, "Commentary on 2 Timothy 1."
21. Hill, "2 Timothy."

CHAPTER 5

The Book of Life

THE THEME OF "THE book of life," which is the subject of two verses in Revelation we want to devote special attention, has roots in both the Old Testament and the New Testament. A bit of background needs to be laid before the next two verses are considered. Ancient Near Eastern kings kept records. For example, Darius stored documents in the house of archives (Ezra 6:1). In addition, Xerxes kept "a book of memorable deeds, the chronicles" (Esth 6:1). In a similar way, King Yahweh is depicted as having a library. But unlike these human kings, King Yahweh has a book in which is written every last day he has decreed for us (Ps 139:16). Every fitful tossing, every shed tear is in God's book (Ps 56:8). Perhaps the best known volume in King Yahweh's library is the book of life.

OLD TESTAMENT

The book of life has roots in both testaments. Moses makes mention of it first in Exod 32. He is interceding for the people of Israel, pleading with God to forgive them. Moses says, "But if not, please blot me out of your book that You have written" (Exod 32:32). From this it is seen that Yahweh has a book that has the names of specific people ("me" refers to Moses) which have been written in the book by Yahweh himself ("You have written").

The Book of Life

David is the first to refer to "the book" as "the book of life." He writes, "May they be blotted out of the book of life/ And may they not be recorded with the righteous" (Ps 69:28, NASB95). David prays this prayer concerning "those who hate me without cause" and "those who would destroy me" (v. 4). Thus, "they" that David prays would be blotted out of the book of life are "those who hate me without cause" and "those who would destroy me." In short, they are David's "enemies" (v. 14, 18), his "foes" (v. 19). David provides a laundry list of their offenses against him, intermingled with imprecations against them (vs. 20-27). At this point, the imprecations reach a crescendo where David petitions God to blot out his enemies' names from God's book of life. The parallel construction of Hebrew poetry indicates that it is "the righteous" whose names are recorded in the book of life. The unrighteous do not have their name in the book of life. Hence, by implication, what awaits the unrighteous is destruction and condemnation from God.

It is not simply because they are David's enemies that they are to be blotted out; rather, it is because they are unrighteous enemies of God that they are blotted out of Yahweh's book of life. Keil and Delitzsch put it concisely: "Let the entrance into God's righteousness, i.e., His justifying and sanctifying grace, be denied to them for ever [sic]."[1] However, Keil and Delitzsch go on to argue that the better translation of the phrase "the book of life" is "the book of the living" (so ESV and LXX). What is in view, then, is that the unrighteous will be removed from "living in this present world."[2] However, the parallel of "the book of life" with "the righteous" points beyond the physical realm and reaches to the spiritual reality. It is the righteous whose names are recorded in the book of life. But it is the unrighteous whose names are blotted out of the book of life. The life in view when it pertains to the book of life is eternal life. The righteous, whose names are written in the book of life, have eternal life. The unrighteous, whose names are blotted out of, that is, are not written in ("not be recorded") the book of life, do not have eternal life.

Daniel also mentions Yahweh's book as he concludes his final vision. Much has been written concerning what exactly Daniel's vision means. Suffice it to say, Daniel predicts a time of unprecedented trouble which would be unlike any other time of distress prior to it. Deliverance from the time of trouble is for "everyone whose name shall be found written in the book"

---

1. Keil and Delitzsch, *Commentary*, 469.
2. Keil and Delitzsch, *Commentary*, 469.

Part I: Redemption Predestined

(Dan 12:1). "In the book"[3] refers to a specific book. By Daniel's time, it has become a common figure for Yahweh's book of life.[4] Noteworthy is that deliverance or salvation is connected to one's having their name written in the book.

As the OT closes, Malachi makes a final veiled reference to the book of life. Malachi presents Yahweh as "a great King" (1:14). Once more King Yahweh is seen to have a book, this time called "a book of remembrance." However, as mentioned above, a book of remembrance for Yahweh is not to help him remember, as though he is a forgetful king. When God "remembers" his people (Noah, Gen 8:1; the people of Israel, Exod 2:24 [esp. noteworthy is the linguistic connection with "heard" in Exodus and how Yahweh "heard" this God-fearing remnant in Malachi's day]), it is for the benefit of his people and for divine action. Indeed, the book that is written is "for[5] those who feared Yahweh," i.e., it is for their benefit, for their assurance that he would "spare them as a man spares his son who serves him" (v. 17).

From the data found in the Old Testament several conclusions can be drawn. First, Yahweh is depicted as having a book which is called "the book of life." Second, Yahweh himself is responsible for writing names in his book or blotting them out. This means Yahweh knows those who are his (cf. 2 Tim 2:19). What is not revealed definitively in the Old Testament is *when* God writes names in his book of life. For that, one must look to the New Testament. Third, having one's name in the book of life is a personal reality which impacts the individual. The righteous person's name is written there while the unrighteous person's name is not written there. Fourth, those whose names are written in Yahweh's book of life know their name is written there. Both Moses and David assume their name is written in the book of life. Fifth, given the parallel construction of Hebrew poetry, to have one's name "blotted out" of the book of life means to have one's name not written in ("not be recorded") the book of life. Again, when the unrighteous person's name is not written in the book of life is not specified in the Old Testament.

---

3. Heb. *bassepher*, with both the preposition (*b*) and the definite article (*h*) attached to the noun (*spr*).

4. Miller, *Daniel*, 315.

5. The Hebrew preposition *l* is attached to the adjective.

The Book of Life

NEW TESTAMENT

Turning to the New Testament one finds continuity and development on the theme of "the book of life." In Phil 4, Paul encourages two sisters to agree in the Lord. He then calls on the church in Philippi, especially a leader there in the church who Paul calls "true companion," to help ameliorate the situation. He writes, "Yes, I ask you also, true companion, help these women, who have labored side by side with me in the gospel together with Clement and the rest of my fellow workers, whose names are in the book of life" (Phil 4:3). Once again one finds the personal nature of the book of life. Eudodia, Syntyche, Clement, "and the rest of my fellow workers" are those "whose names are in the book of life." Each of these individuals have their name written in the book of life. Further, they can know their names are written in the book of life, bringing assurance.

Revelation is the book of the Bible which has the most references to the book of life. In Jesus' epistle to Sardis, he promises "the one who conquers . . . I will never blot his name out of the book of life" (3:5). The word for "blot" is the same verb which translates the Hebrew word "blot" used by Moses in Exod 32:32.[6] Jesus promises his church, even the individual members who overcome, that he will "never" blot out their name. Again, the personal nature of the Lord's knowledge of his people is clear. He knows each one by name.

It is essential that a person's name be written in the book of life. If it is not, their destiny is in the lake of fire. This is taught near the end of Revelation. In the vision of the great white throne judgment John writes, "And I saw the dead, great and small, standing before the throne, and books were opened. Then another book was opened, which is the book of life. And the dead were judged by what was written in the books, according to what they had done" (Rev 20:12). The most difficult aspect for proper interpretation of this passage (vs. 11–15) is recognizing that this is a judgment scene. God's people, though, do not come into judgment. Indeed, the one who hears Jesus' word and believes Christ "has eternal life." "He does not come into judgment, but has passed from death to life" (John 5:24). Therefore, the great white throne judgment is for "the dead" (v. 12, 13), i.e., those do not have life.[7]

---

6. Gk. *exaleiphō*

7. Hoyt says that the judgment scene depicted in Rev 20:11–15 is "the judgment of the unsaved *dead*" (*Judgment Seat of Christ*, 32. Emphasis original). Hoyt's thesis is that the judgment seat of Christ which believers will stand before for reward is different than

Part I: Redemption Predestined

"Dead" is used to describe the state of the individual spiritually, not necessarily physically. This comes into clearer focus in the context. First, "the sea gave up the dead who were in it" (v. 13a). Uniformly throughout the Revelation "the sea" has been a prophetic image for nations.[8] So from among the nations—every tribe, language, people—there are spiritually dead people over whom Death reigns (cf. Rom 5:14). As long as a person remains in their trespasses and sins, they remain dead. Second, "Death and Hades gave up the dead who were in them" (v. 13b). If all that is meant by "the dead" is physical death, then one would expect only Hades to be mentioned, since everyone who dies ends up in the unseen realm of disembodied spirits (i.e., hades). However, both Death and Hades are mentioned, both being personified here, indicated by the use of capital letters in the English translation. Elsewhere in the New Testament, Paul personifies Sin and Death in Rom 5:12ff. "Death reigned from Adam to Moses," writes Paul. Death is pictured as a tyrant, reigning over fallen humanity. In fact, Death seems to be a vassal of Sin since Paul writes, "Sin reigned in Death" (5:21). John seems to be similarly picturing Death and Hades as twin tyrants, one ruling over the spiritually dead who are living (Death), the other reigning over the spiritually dead who have died (Hades). If this is the case, then "the dead" are the whole lot of unsaved humanity, those whose names are not written in the book of life. They are raised to stand before the great white throne for judgment, viz., the second death.

Next one reads about "books" being opened. The picture here is that each person has a book s/he is writing which will be opened at the judgment. This echoes a scene from Daniel where books are opened when the divine court sits in judgment (Dan 7:9–10). In Revelation, these books contain all the deeds of humans. Each of "the dead" is judged based on the record contained in their book, that is, "what was written in the books." The judgment of every person is "according to what they had done," their deeds having been written in their respective book. "They were judged, each one of them, according to what they had done," says John. They stand before the great white throne with only their naked, imperfect works. At the same time, "another book" is opened which is identified as "the book of life." The inclusion of a person's name in the book of life is *not according*

---

the judgment unbelievers will face at the great white throne judgment. While I do not agree with all of Hoyt's conclusions the distinction in the judgments seems valid.

8. This is typical prophetic imagery. E.g., Ps 65:7; Isa 17:12; 57:20; Jer 6:23; 49:23; 51:36, 42; Ezek 26:3; Dan 7:2–3.

to what they had done. This will be developed further when 13:8 and 17:8 are further explicated.

There are other allusions elsewhere in the Bible which speak to people or their names being recorded or written in a heavenly record. Isaiah explains how "everyone who has been recorded for life in Jerusalem" will be called holy following the purifying judgment of God visited upon Zion (Isa 4:3). Jesus himself exhorts his disciples to rejoice because "your names are written in heaven" (Luke 10:20). The perfect passive verb for "written" indicates that it is God, not the disciples, who wrote their names in heaven (passive voice) and that it was written at some point in the past and stands written in heaven (perfect tense).

NAMES WRITTEN AND THE LAMB SLAIN BEFORE THE CREATION OF THE WORLD

All of the foregoing has bearing upon verses in the Revelation where "the book of life" is mentioned. Three verses which make mention of the book of life have been dealt with briefly already (3:5; 20:12, 15). The other two verses in the Revelation which mention the book of life further impress the fact of the divine intention to redeem a particular people prior to creation: 13:8 and 17:8. The first, Rev 13:8, has the difficulty of the possibility of being translated in one of two ways. The ESV reads:

> and all who dwell on earth will worship it, everyone whose name has not been written before the foundation of the world in the book of life of the Lamb who was slain. (Rev 13:8)

In this rendering the writing of the names in the Lamb's book of life is what takes place "before the foundation of the world" (The NASB reads similarly). So in eternity, the Father writes the names of his elect people in the book of life which belongs to his Son, the Lamb. Or, in eternity, in agreement with what the Father has written in the book of life, it is determined the Son will be slain for them. This latter understanding is reflected in the alternate rendering found in the NIV:

> All inhabitants of the earth will worship the beast—all whose names have not been written in the book of life belonging to the Lamb that was slain from the creation of the world. (Rev 13:8, NIV84)

Part I: Redemption Predestined

In this rendering the atoning sacrifice of Christ (the Lamb) is what is in view "from the creation of the world." The meaning is that "the death of Christ was a redemptive sacrifice decreed in the counsels of eternity."[9] This view has much going for it since the antecedent of "from the creation of the world" is "the Lamb that was slain" in the original language. It is the natural way of understanding the phrase given this is the original word order.

Leaving the difficulty aside, it can be affirmed that the beast worshipping earth dwellers do not have their names written in the Lamb's book of life. These stand in contrast with God's people who are called "those who dwell in heaven" (13:6) and "saints" (13:7). The beast and his followers make war against God and his followers. These two camps are divided into those whose names have never been recorded in the Lamb's book of life and those whose names are written in the book of life.

The other text in Revelation which offers additional insight concerning the book of life and which may also help clarify the difficulty in 13:8 is found just a few chapters later:

> The beast that you saw was, and is not, and is about to rise from the bottomless pit and go to destruction. And the dwellers on earth whose names have not been written in the book of life from the foundation of the world will marvel to see the beast, because it was and is not and is to come. (Rev 17:8)

Here the phrase "of the Lamb who was slain" is not present. This provides a clear statement as to when the names of "the dwellers on earth" were not written and continue to be unwritten. Their names were not written "from the foundation of the world," and this condition persists. Thus, the phrase "whose names have not been written in the book of life from the foundation of the world" negatively affirms that the names of "the dwellers on earth," i.e., beast worshippers (13:7–8), were never recorded in the book of life.

Conversely, the names of Christ's people ("saints," 13:7) are positively identified later as "those who are written in the Lamb's book of life" (21:27). Given everything covered thus far in previous chapters—the Father chose us in Christ in eternity (Ephesians 1:4), the Father giving us his purpose and grace in Christ before time began (2 Tim 1:9), the Father loving those he gives to the Son in the same way he loves the Son (John 17:23–24)—it seems reasonable to conclude that when names were written in the book of life is "before the foundation of the world." So whether "before the

---

9. Mounce, *Revelation*, 252.

foundation of the world" in 13:8 is understood following the normal word order modifying "the Lamb that was slain" or is understood as modifying "written in the book of life," 17:8 affirmatively demonstrates that names of individuals are written or not in the book of life "before/from the foundation of the world."

Here is the answer to the question left unanswered by the Old Testament: when are names written in the book of life? The timestamp for when God writes names in his book is "before the foundation of the world." We can go further: just as it was decreed that the Lamb would be slain so that by his blood he would ransom people for God from every tribe, language, people, and nation (Rev 5:9), so it was decreed that the Lamb would be slain for all those whose names are written in the book of life. Indeed, the names written in the Lamb's book of life represent individuals from every tribe, language, nation, and people.

Part II

Redemption Accomplished

In eternity, "before the foundation of the world," the Father foreknew the Son as the Lamb without spot or blemish whose precious blood would ransom people for God. In the fullness of time, the Son "was made manifest in the last times for the sake of you" (1 Pet 1:20). The redemption that was predestined by the Father in the Son according to the Spirit is accomplished by the Son on the cross in history.

The accomplishment of redemption through Christ on the cross is territory which is a bit more familiar for most Christians. Christ's cross is the subject of many a sermon and Bible class. What may not be as familiar to us is how the cross and the accomplished redemption by Christ thereon is situated within a Trinitarian framework.

The accomplishment of redemption in history is the particular work of the Son. It is the Son, not the Father nor the Spirit, who becomes flesh, takes on human nature, and dies on the cross. At the same time, the work of the Son is not isolated from the Father nor the Spirit. God sends God to die for sinners. The Son obeys the Father by the Spirit in coming into the world ("born of woman"), living the sinless life we could never live, and dying the death that was due us. Christ died in our place on the cross, thereby satisfying the wrath of the Father upon sins. The death of Christ on the cross is the fulfillment of the divine will from eternity.

The centrality of the glory of the triune God is evident in the Pauline phrase "the gospel of the glory of Christ, who is the image of God" and "the glory of God in the face of Jesus Christ" (2 Cor 4:4, 6).

Chapter 6

The Son Offers Himself Through the Spirit to the Father to Obtain Eternal Redemption

Hebrews 9 begins with a review of the "first covenant," i.e., the Levitical sacrificial system (v. 1–10). The things which made up the service and system of that first covenant were indicators by the Holy Spirit that throne room access for the saints was not yet (v. 8). However, there was a "time of reformation" coming which would bring about a new order, a change in things. Christ ushers in that time of change:

> But when Christ appeared as a high priest of the good things that have come, then through the greater and more perfect tent (not made with hands, that is, not of this creation) he entered once for all into the holy places, not by means of the blood of goats and calves but by means of his own blood, thus securing an eternal redemption. For if the blood of goats and bulls, and the sprinkling of defiled persons with the ashes of a heifer, sanctify for the purification of the flesh, how much more will the blood of Christ, who through the eternal Spirit offered himself without blemish to God, purify our conscience from dead works to serve the living God. (Heb 9:11–14)

Part II: Redemption Accomplished

The identity of the new covenant high priest is specifically named as Christ, or Messiah. "Christ appeared" accentuates his time on earth when he was manifested in the flesh. Christ appeared, having been sent by the Father, to accomplish the will of the Father (John 4:34; Christ says he came to accomplish the work of him who sent him, i.e., the Father). It was in the flesh and through his flesh that Christ brought into reality "good things." In saying the good things "have come," the writer points to the fact that through the work of Christ the good things pertaining to salvation and redemption have been realized through the Son's fulfillment of the Father's will. Both participles are aorist tense, indicating the whole incarnation of the Son of God, viz., his life, ministry, and death—the whole work of the Son which the Father sent him to do. Christ accomplished the work, and thereby the good things are realized.

It is "through the greater and more perfect tent" which is not handmade, that is, "not of this creation," by which Christ entered the holy places. This "tent" is his body, his flesh. When it is remembered that John wrote, "The Word became flesh and tabernacled/tented among us," there using the verbal form while the writer of Hebrews uses the noun in 9:11b, the picture comes into view. During his circus trial, false witnesses said, "We heard him say, 'I will destroy this temple that is made with hands, and in three days I will build another, not made with hands'" (Mark 14:58). Yet another aspect comes into view. For while the false witnesses clearly misrepresent the words of Christ, the writer of Hebrews, moved by the Holy Spirit, provides a clear understanding: Christ's tent, "not made with hands," is his body. So the human nature of Christ is "greater" in dignity and worth than the old tabernacle. In addition, the human nature of Christ is "more perfect" in being suited to fulfill the old tabernacle and make atonement for sin. Further, it is "not made with hands" which stands in contrast with the tabernacle and temple under the old covenant which was made with human hands. This may also point to the conception of Christ since he was conceived by the power of the Holy Spirit (Luke 1:31, 35). Finally, it is "not of this creation" in that while the body of Christ was certainly of the same substance as ours (the author will mention his blood in the next verse), it was the product of divine power and of divine origin, without aid of this creation. This is pictured prophetically and quoted by the writer in 10:5: "a body you have prepared for Me" (citing Ps 40:6). It is "through" this tent that Christ entered the holy places.

The Son Offers Himself Through the Spirit to the Father

"He entered," which signals the entrance of the Messiah into "the holy places," wherein is the presence of God, is the main verb. "He entered" is aorist tense and coupled with "once for all" (a temporal adverb), highlights the finished work of redemption by Christ. Christ as high priest offered sacrifice for the sins of his people once for all when he offered himself (7:27). "When Christ had offered for all time a single sacrifice for sins, He sat down at the right hand of God," even God the Father (10:12). The Son accomplished the work of the Father in redeeming people from sin by his sacrifice for their sins. Then, the Son sat down at the right hand of the Father in heaven, resting from his finished work.

In contrast with the old priesthood which required repetition year-in and year-out, Christ's sacrifice is singular and requires no repetition. Further, Christ entered the heavenly holiest of holies after his sacrifice, thereby fulfilling the type of the high priest under the sacrificial system who would kill the sacrifice and then enter the holy place with the blood of the sacrifice (e.g., Lev 16:15–16). It is "not by means of the blood of goats and calves," as was prescribed under the Law. Once more the greater and more perfect work of Christ is evident when Christ entered the holy place "by means of His own blood." As the high priest entered the most holy place once a year "not without taking blood" (9:7), so Christ entered the heavenly holy place once for all "by means of His own blood."

The challenge for Christians today is to maintain the full orbed view the writer of Hebrews has of Christ's high priestly work. Because many Christians are not as familiar with the Hebrew Scriptures as they ought to be, there is a tendency to flatten out Christ's work. The sacrifice of Christ took place on the cross, where he shed his blood and perfectly fulfilled the will of Father. He accomplished the work of redemption on the cross. Hence, he says as he dies, "It is finished" (John 19:30). At the same time, after the resurrection and ascension, Jesus entered into the heavenly holy place with his resurrected body and "by means of His own blood." In this triumphal entrance of the Son of God into the Father's presence he thereby secures eternal redemption. So from the perspective of the writer of Hebrews, Christ's entire work, similar to but greater than the high priest under the old covenant on the Day of Atonement, is viewed as whole: from cross through ascension to entrance into heaven.

Following his resurrection Christ ascended into heaven where he presented himself before the Father as our eternal redeemer and great high priest. "The holy places" (9:12) which Christ entered correspond to "heaven

Part II: Redemption Accomplished

itself" (9:24; cf. 8:2). Whereas "the holy places" (i.e., the most holy place) were "made with hands" under the first covenant, heaven is not of human origin. Indeed, it is the dwelling place "of the true things," especially the glory and majesty of God. This he enters as our living, eternal high priest, having secured eternal redemption by his blood and having conquered sin, death, hell, and Satan by his cross (cf. Col 2:14–15).

Christ does not offer himself again in heaven. "He always lives to make intercession" for those whom he saves (7:25). The sacrifice upon the altar of the cross precedes the presentation of the Son in the presence of the Father. His sacrificial work for redemption was accomplished on the cross. Just as the sin offering was slaughtered "before Yahweh" and then the blood taken into the tent of meeting (cf. Lev 4:4–5, 15–16; 16:11, 14, 15), so also Christ sheds his blood on the cross and then, upon his ascension, enters into the heavenly holy places one time for all time. So the entrance of Christ into the presence of his Father was triumphant since he entered heaven by virtue of his sacrifice ("*by means of [dia]* His own blood"). It is because of his perfect sacrifice that our redemption is secured forever, and he triumphantly enters into the heavenly holy places to be our Mediator forever.

The effect of the blood of Christ is seen in the phrase "thus securing eternal redemption" or "having obtained eternal redemption" (NASB). The blood of the Son shed on the cross and presented before the Father in the heavenly holy places secured or obtained eternal redemption. "Redemption" is a release or to be set free and assumes slavery. Verse 15 mentions redemption from transgressions, i.e., sins. Sin is the reason people need redemption. So on the cross by means of his blood, Christ is purchasing people from slavery to the bondage of sin (since his sacrifice was for sins, 10:12). The redemption is "eternal" because it is complete (nothing lacking), applies for all time ("once for all"), is unrepeatable, and points to the final end of Christ "bringing many sons to glory" to the glory of the Father (2:10). This eternal redemption is secured or obtained by Christ. There is nothing prospective or potential about the eternal redemption Christ secures. Christ actually obtains the eternal redemption of the children given to the Son by the Father (cf. 2:13).

Christ's high priestly work is presented here as a singular whole. That is, his offering of himself on the cross thereby shedding his blood for his people *and* his presentation of himself in the heavenly holy places on behalf of his people by means of his blood is a single work. This corresponds to the high priest's single work under the Law: both the slaughter of the animal *and*

The Son Offers Himself Through the Spirit to the Father

the presentation of the animal's blood (i.e., its life) were necessary to make atonement. Sacrifice, then presentation. The priest's work was not completed with the shedding of blood; presentation of that blood in the holy place was necessary. Nor could he present what had not been sacrificed. Hence, Christ being our great high priest, it was necessary for him to both sacrifice himself on the cross *and* ascend back to the Father in order to enter the heavenly holy places by his own blood. It is through this whole work that Christ obtains eternal redemption and "the promised eternal inheritance" for "those who are called" (9:15), i.e., Christ's "brothers," "the children God has given Me," and "the offspring of Abraham" (2:11, 13, 16).

The price for this eternal redemption is Christ, even his blood shed on the cross. This also explains why the redemption he secures is eternal: the eternal Son of God offered himself. More specifically, eternal redemption is obtained by the eternal Son offering his blood through the eternal Spirit to the eternal Father. Here is the Trinitarian harmony in the redemption of people.

Given the nature of the sacrifice (the blood of God the Son), the infinite value of the redemption comes into view. Since the sacrifice of the eternal Son is of infinite value, it is sufficient to redeem not only our world but many worlds. The sufficiency of the sacrifice is one thing. The efficiency of the sacrifice is another. While the sacrifice of the eternal Son is sufficient for many worlds, it is efficient only for "the sins of many" (9:28), i.e., "the children God has given Me" (2:13b). These are "those who draw near to God through Christ" whom Christ is able to save completely and for whom he makes intercession (7:25). They also are "those who are called" to receive the promised inheritance (9:15). So the blood of Christ effectively ransoms people for God from the world over, "from every tribe and language and people and nation" (Rev 5:9), and from all time and history.

Verses 13–14 offer a comparison between the sacrificial system of the old covenant and the new covenant sacrifice of Christ. Once more the greater or better nature of Christ's work as high priest and sacrifice are manifest. "For" builds on the argument from the previous two verses. "How much more" highlights the efficacy of Christ's sacrifice in comparison to the old covenant sacrifices. It is a lesser to greater argument, the lesser being the ordinances under the first covenant, the greater being Christ's offering of himself. The bloody sacrifices of goats and calves effectively sanctified defiled persons "for the purification of the flesh" (v. 13). Fleshly defilement was purified so that the defiled person could enter into communal worship of God. This was the limited value of the ritual purification of the Jewish system.

"The blood of goats and calves" is the writer's way of referencing back to the Day of Atonement which he had already referenced in verse 7 ("the high priest goes. . .but once a year" into the Most Holy Place [9:7]; see Lev 16). The plural "goats and calves" is likely indicating the annual repetition of the Day of Atonement, something he will refer to later (10:3, "year by year"). This writer also mentions "the ashes of a heifer" which refers to the sacrifice of an unblemished red heifer to produce a purification solution (Num 19). This was not an annual sacrifice and is likely marshalled as a summary of all the rites of purification under the Law. Reference to both the Day of Atonement and the red heifer ordinance may be intended to operate as a summary of the entire sacrificial system, both concerning atonement and purification. However, it seems better to recognize that both the sacrifices on the Day of Atonement as well as the red heifer sprinkling were called sin offerings (Lev 16:5, 9, 11; Num 19:9).

The effect of these sin offerings, as with every sin offering under the first covenant, was to "sanctify for the purification of the flesh." The "defiled person" was made holy with the goal of ritual external purification. This cleansing was a good thing since it enabled the worshiper to draw near to God whereas so long as defilement remained they were excluded from such activity.

The superiority of the efficacy of Christ's blood is drawn from the phrase "how much more" and the effects Christ's blood has on his people, viz., purification of the conscience (v. 14). In addition, it is the triune God who is at work in atonement and redemption. Christ, the eternal Son, in all his holy, unblemished perfection, "offered Himself" through the eternal Spirit to God, i.e., the eternal Father. We contribute nothing to the work of atonement except defiled and impure consciences full of dead works. "Dead works" are either works that lead to death or works that are dead because they are performed by those who are spiritually dead.[1] These dead works performed by those dead in trespasses and sins further accentuates the holy, life-giving work of "the living God." The triune God perfectly accomplishes eternal redemption, eternal salvation (5:9).

Christ through the eternal Spirit offered himself without blemish to God. Christ as God presents himself to God through God. The accomplishment of redemption is through-and-through the work of God. Also, there

---

1. Allen, *Hebrews*, 473.

The Son Offers Himself Through the Spirit to the Father

is a singular intention of God in the atonement. The Father, the Son, and the Holy Spirit work in harmonious concert in accomplishing the work of eternal redemption. As seen, in eternity the Father chose people whom he gave to the Son. The Father then sends the Son, the Son coming willingly into the world, to die for the redemption of the people given to him by the Father. The Son willingly lays down his life on the cross, shedding his blood for the sins of the people. Through the Holy Spirit the Son presents himself, even his blood, to the Father on behalf of his people. In this the triune God secures the eternal redemption of his people.

The "eternal Spirit" is the Holy Spirit. "Through the eternal Spirit" points to the efficiency of the Son's offering. Without the Holy Spirit, the offering of the Son would have been ineffectual. How exactly the writer intends for us to understand the role of the Spirit in the sacrifice of Christ is not clear. There is nothing concrete in the gospels concerning the Holy Spirit at the cross. However, a few possibilities arise. One possibility is that as the Spirit led the Son of God into the wilderness to be tempted by the devil, so it may be that the Spirit led him to the cross. In this way, we see the Son dependent upon the resources of the Spirit in his death. Another possibility is that the Holy Spirit-inspired word is on the lips of Christ as he dies. Psalm 22 is on his lips as he dies (Matt 26:46, "My God, My God, etc."). Also, "Father, into Your hands I commit My Spirit" is from Ps 31:5 (Luke 23:46). Moffitt offers a third possibility, where the resurrection of Christ is the work of the eternal Spirit.[2] However, the depths of this divine mystery are beyond our comprehension.

It is "to God" that Christ offered himself. The Son offered himself to the Father. God the Father is here presented as lawgiver and judge to whom the Son offers himself as satisfaction for the transgressions of the people against the Law (9:15). The efficacy of the sacrifice is evident in the one sacrificed (the Son), the agent through whom the sacrifice is made (the Spirit), and one to whom the sacrifice is offered (the Father). It accomplishes the purpose for which it is offered (purification of the conscience, eternal redemption) because it is the triune God who executes it.

---

2. Moffitt, *Rethinking the Atonement*, 144n19.

CHAPTER 7

Propitiation

The Son Satisfies the Father's Wrath

IN THE MIDDLE OF the 20th century, Leon Morris wrote about a tendency in his day by some who sought to overlook or explain away God's wrath.[1] This same tendency remains to the present. There are those who want to explain away or, if possible, delete entirely the wrath of God from the pages of the Bible. However, such a task requires a radical re-envisioning of not only the entire Scripture but of the Trinity as well.

The Scriptures ubiquitously and consistently teach that God has wrath.[2] For example, the psalmist writes, "O God, you have rejected us, broken our defenses; you have been angry; oh, restore us. You have made the land to quake; you have torn it open; repair its breaches, for it totters. You have made your people see hard things; you have given us wine to drink that made us stagger" (Ps 60:1–3). Several points are worth noting which are typical of the wrath of God. First, David, the penmen of this psalm, addresses God as "God," not using the divine name (Yahweh). Psalms of lament, such as Ps 60 is, generally follow this pattern and indicates humiliation and affliction of soul, as though the psalmist is so burdened by his sin that he cannot address God by his name but simply as God. Second, this was a psalm to be sung by the choir in worship and collectively by

---

1. Morris, *Apostolic Preaching*, 174.
2. Morris reviews the biblical data from the OT and NT concerning the wrath of God (*Apostolic Preaching*, 147–54, 179–84).

the people of Israel. It is "us" whom God has rejected, torn, and made to see hard things. What is true of the individual writer is likewise true for the people corporately: troubled by sin, in their humiliation, they can only address God as "God." Third, God is personally active in his wrath. "You have been angry," goes the psalm. "You" here is unmistakably God, even Yahweh the God of Israel. He is the subject of the verb "angry." This is not an impersonal wrath nor wrath by proxy. God himself has wrath and then acts according to his righteous and holy anger. He personally rejects his sinful people. He personally breaks their defenses. He personally causes the land to quake so that it tears open. He personally caused his people to experience hardship. He made them to drink from the cup of his divine wrath.[3]

THE WRATH OF GOD THE FATHER

Coming to the NT, the Father sends the Son, who perfectly reveals the Father. God the Son consistently taught that his Father in heaven has wrath against sinners. He taught about a man who owned a vineyard that he leased to tenants who beat and killed his servants before killing the vineyard owner's son.[4] As a result the vineyard owner would "destroy those tenants" (Luke 20:16). So clear is his teaching that even those who heard him utter the parable conclude that the vineyard owner will "put those wretches to a miserable death" (Matt 21:41). Most interpreters of this parable take the vineyard owner to be the Father who ultimately sends his Son who is killed by the tenants that represent the Jewish people. If such an interpretation attains, then it is the Father who pours out his wrath upon the nation of Israel for their sin.

What is taught symbolically in parables is reinforced through direct teaching. "Whoever believes in the Son has eternal life; whoever does not obey the Son shall not see life, but the wrath of God remains on him" (John 3:36). There is discussion about whether John the Baptist's words stop at verse 30 or if they continue to the end of the chapter. Either option is possible. Whether these are the words of John the Baptist or the apostle John, through the Spirit John is revealing the Father's settled disposition toward

---

3. "Wine to drink" is an allusion to the cup of divine wrath Yahweh possesses which he causes sinful people/nations to drink to the dregs before he brings judgment and calamity upon them (see Isa 52:17, 22; Jer 25:15–17).

4. This parable is found in the synoptic gospels: Matt 21:33–44; Mark 12:1–12; Luke 20:9–18.

those who reject the Son. Rejection of the Son leaves one under the wrath of the Father.

THE WRATH OF GOD THE SON

Not only does the Father have wrath toward sin, but so too the Son has wrath. In Revelation, God the Son is figuratively portrayed as a Lamb (5:6, 12–13). Chapter six of the vision sees several seals opened. As cataclysmic geographic and stellar events take place, all kinds of people are seen fleeing, hiding themselves in caves and mountains, calling upon the mountains to collapse on them to "hide us from the face of Him who sits on the throne, and the wrath of the Lamb, for the great day of their wrath has come" (Rev 6:15–17). The Trinitarian nature of the wrath of God stands out boldly in the phrase "their wrath." This is the wrath of him who sits on the throne and the Lamb, i.e., the Father and the Son. Both the Father and the Son have wrath toward all those who abide under sin.

Indeed, it will be the Son who treads "the winepress of the fury of the wrath of God the Almighty" (Rev 19:15). This imagery is derived from Isa 63:1–6, where the Savior of Israel, Yahweh (62:11), is returning from Edom in crimson garments.[5] His garments are red because "their lifeblood spattered on My garments and stained all My apparel" (v. 3b). "I have trodden the winepress alone," he announces, "I trod them in My anger and trampled them in My wrath" (v. 3a). In Revelation, John sees King Jesus engaging in the same work as Yahweh, a not-so-subtle hint at his deity. The various accompanying weapons of war (sword and rod, which are themselves allusive to Isa 49:2 and Ps 2:9, respectively), as well as the mention of God's furious wrath are indicators that when the Son treads the winepress, he does so in the same disposition as Yahweh: "In My anger . . . in My wrath." Behold, the wrath of the Son!

---

5. The allusion to Isa 63:1–6 in Rev 19:15 is seen in several linguistic and thematic links between the LXX and the NT text: (1) the same word for "winepress" (*lēnon* [Isa 63:2]) is used in the LXX and by John; (2) both texts mention God's "wrath" (*thunou* [Isa 63:3]); (3) the objects of divine wrath are "the nations" (root: *ethnos* [Isa 63:3]); (4) both texts describe clothes (*himation* [Isa 63:2; Rev 19:13]) dipped in "blood" (root: *haima* [Isa 63:3, 6; Rev 19:13]); (5) both actions are undertaken as judgment upon rebellious nations.

THE WRATH OF GOD THE HOLY SPIRIT

The wrath of the Spirit is less explicit in Scripture. However, it does appear in Isa 63. The people of Israel were saved by "their Savior" (v. 8; cf. 62:11), i.e., Yahweh. But the people rebelled against him (v. 10). Their rebellion "grieved His Holy Spirit." This resulted in "He [the Holy Spirit] turned to be their enemy and Himself fought against them" (Isa 63:10). It is as a wrathful enemy that the Holy Spirit fights against the rebellious house of Israel. This adds background and color to the warning from Paul in Ephesians: "do not grieve the Holy Spirit of God" (4:30). Those who grieve God's Holy Spirit end up with a wrathful enemy fighting against them.

THE WRATH OF THE TRINITY

The entire Bible affirms the wrath of God. God personally has wrath toward sin and sinners. The Father has wrath. The Son has wrath. The Holy Spirit has wrath. The triune God has wrath, and this wrath abides on sinners for their sin. With this foundation, attention can be given to what the triune God has done to appease or turn away his wrath.

There are those who would deny that God has wrath. God being wrathful is too pagan, either unworthy of God or else repugnant. Moo replies to the objection that God having wrath is pagan in conception. First, "God's wrath is the inevitable and necessary reaction of absolute holiness to sin," which stands in distinct contrast with the capricious pagan deities. Second, God himself provides propitiation, even *is* propitiation, whereas pagan deities are merely rendered willing to forgive through expiation.[6] As established above, Scripture depicts God's settled disposition to sin as wrath. But Scripture also presents God as satisfying his own wrath as propitiation.

Others might object that God having wrath is too human. Wrath is uncontrolled or irrational passion. If there is wrath in the divine nature, then God is subject to outbursts like a human. However, such an anthropomorphic characterization is foreign to Scripture. God is slow to anger, and the notion of uncontrolled passion is not necessary for the wrath of God. Further, Scripture depicts God's wrath as "a burning zeal for right coupled with a perfect hatred for everything that is evil."[7] Such wrath is reasonable and right for God.

---

6. Moo, *Romans*, 235–36.
7. Morris, *Apostolic Preaching*, 209.

Part II: Redemption Accomplished

DEFINING PROPITIATION

God's wrath is taught consistently throughout the Bible. The big Bible word for the satisfaction or turning away of God's wrath is "propitiation." Propitiation is God's response to his own wrath. Its basic definition is "to appease, to placate, to avert wrath."[8] It means "the removal of wrath."[9] It is the means by which sins are forgiven, the means of forgiveness, an atoning sacrifice. The word has reference to the one party who is propitiated by the sacrifice made. In the New Testament, God is propitiated by the sacrifice of Jesus Christ the righteous. Christ is pictured as the one offered/sacrificed for our sins. The turning away or satisfaction of wrath is due to Christ Jesus. John Owen identifies four essential elements of propitiation:

> In the use of this word, then, there is always understood,—[1st.] An *offence*, crime, guilt, or debt, to be taken away; [2dly.] A *person offended*, to be pacified, atoned, reconciled; [3dly.] A *person offending*, to be pardoned, accepted; [4thly.] A *sacrifice* or other means of making the atonement. Sometimes one is expressed, sometimes another, but the use of the word hath respect unto them all.[10]

Following Owen, then, and applying it to the New Testament concept of propitiation we can identify the four categories. The offense that needs to be taken away is *sin*. The person offended by the sin who needs to be pacified is *God*, viz., the Father. The person who has perpetrated the offense and needs to be pardoned is the *sinner*. Finally, the sacrifice for pacifying God and making atonement is *Christ*, viz., God the Son.

From this one can see the clear difference between pagan notions of propitiation and the biblical view. While both views recognize divine wrath, the nature of that wrath is vastly different (monotheistic and Trinitarian versus polytheistic). Further, the means and results of propitiation are likewise different. The pagan himself offered the gift in order to change the deities mind, bribing his god in an effort to cause the god(s) to look favorably upon him. According to Scripture, God himself is the only appropriate sacrifice to satisfy his own wrath so that people can come to him.[11] Finally, there is also the idea of substitution, which is unique to Scripture. It is understood that either I retain my sins and thereby remain under the wrath of God or

---

8. Lloyd-Jones, *Romans*, 70.
9. Morris, *Romans*, 180.
10. Owen, *Hebrews*, 476. Emphasis original.
11. Morris, *Apostolic Preaching*, 210–11.

else the Son of God takes upon himself the wrath of God for our sins. Either Christ dies for our sins, or we die in our sins. It is Christ's life for our life. "Either we die or He dies."[12] Clearly, the biblical conception of propitiation is as different than the pagan notion as light is different than darkness.

As established, God's settled disposition toward evil and sin is wrath. Due to sin people are under the wrath of God. Yet we also know that God loves the world (John 3:16). Under the old covenant, God gave the blood of bulls and goats for his people on the altar "to make atonement for your souls" (Lev 17:11). This anticipated what God would do in the NT; God takes the initiative and sends his unique Son to be propitiation for our sins and the sins of the whole world. So God's wrath needed to be propitiated; God's love did the propitiating. "It is God himself who in holy wrath needs to be propitiated, God himself who in holy love undertook to do the propitiating and God himself who in the person of his Son died for the propitiation of our sins."[13] God put forward himself in the person of Jesus Christ, the Son of God, as propitiation (wrath satisfaction) by his blood. So long as we remain uncovered by his blood due to our disobedience/rebellion, we remain under his wrath. But when we believe and obey God and are covered by Christ's blood, we escape God's holy wrath.

Leon Morris summarizes succinctly the matter when he writes about the seeming paradox of propitiation. On the one hand, God's wrath is upon sinners. On the other hand, God himself removes that wrath. God provides the means of satisfying his own wrath. While it may seem paradoxical, "it accounts for the facts."[14]

PROPITIATION IN THE NEW TESTAMENT

The remainder of this chapter will examine the New Testament references to propitiation: Rom 3:25; Heb 2:17; 1 John 2:2; 4:10.

Romans 3:24–25

Romans 3:19–20 summarizes Paul's argument in his epistle to the Romans thus far which began in 1:18: the whole world—Jew and gentile—is

---

12. Morris, *Apostolic Preaching*, 213.
13. Stott, *Cross of Christ*, 172.
14. Morris, *Romans*, 180n127.

Part II: Redemption Accomplished

accountable to God for their sin, the Law (Torah) doing what it was designed to do in bringing knowledge of sin and condemning the whole world of sin before God ("no human being will be justified in His sight," 3:20). Verse 21 commences the next section with a shift from universal condemnation to something new, expressed in the phrase "but now," namely, the glory of the gospel. The gospel presented here (vs. 21–31) by Paul is Trinitarian since it is "the righteousness of God" accomplished "in Christ Jesus." That is, those in God the Son have the righteousness of God the Father. Indeed, the righteousness of the Son is the righteousness of the Father, since righteousness is inherent in the being of God, all three persons sharing in that one being.

Paul affirms his conclusion again in that "all," that is, Jews and gentiles, "have sinned and fall short of the glory of God." Then Paul writes:

> and are justified by his grace as a gift, through the redemption that is in Christ Jesus, whom God put forward as a propitiation by his blood, to be received by faith. This was to show God's righteousness, because in his divine forbearance he had passed over former sins. (Rom 3:24–25)

The focal point of this passage is the phrase "whom God put forward." "Christ Jesus" is the one "God put forward" in order to accomplish justification, redemption, and propitiation. The emphasis is on Christ doing what humans cannot do. Humans cannot justify themselves before God. Humans cannot redeem themselves. Humans cannot propitiate God. But Christ is publicly displayed (cf. NASB) and set forth by God himself as the means of justification, redemption, and propitiation.

Paul writes that Christians are "justified." James White in his comprehensive study of the subject of justification argues against the idea of "subjective change or provisional status with God" as the meaning of justification. He writes, "Instead, the focus is solely upon God. Justification is his gracious and free declaration, and it is made possible solely because of the redemptive work of Christ."[15] In commenting on the word "being justified," Moo explains, "As Paul uses it in these contexts, the verb 'justify' means not 'to make righteous' (in an ethical sense) nor simply 'to treat as righteous' (though one is really not righteous), but 'to declare righteous.'"[16] Whatever charges might be brought against a person due to their sins have been dropped because of what God did in Christ.

---

15. White, *God Who Justifies*, 190.
16. Moo, *Romans*, 227.

Propitiation

It must be observed that justification is "by His grace," i.e., by God's grace. The unmerited nature of being declared righteous is accentuated in this phrase. Justification is also "as a gift" or "freely." Being justified by God is unearned and is to be received as a gift. God's freedom in giving the gracious gift of his justification as well as the receiver's inability to do anything to earn or deserve the gift are both clearly in view. Finally, the meritorious cause of justification is "the redemption that is in Christ Jesus." The Father's declaration of Christians as righteous and acquitting us of charges is "through" Christ's redeeming work on the cross. Redemption assumes a state of captivity or bondage. All people are in slavery to sin (cf. 3:9). Christ the redeemer, in order to free his people from their sins, bore their sins in his body on the tree so as to take away sin.

Verse 25 further explains the nature of the redemptive work of Christ Jesus as propitiation. God puts forward Christ the redeemer as propitiation. In other words, the Father sets forth the Son as propitiation. As a result of sin, "the wrath of God is being revealed from heaven against all ungodliness and unrighteousness of men" (1:18). Thus, "all, both Jews and Greeks, are under sin" (3:9), and therefore, all are under wrath. Paul reaffirms "all have sinned and fall short of the glory of God" (3:23). God's settled disposition to sin is wrath. Since there is sin, there is wrath. And since there is wrath, propitiation is needed.

God the Father puts forward his Son, Jesus Christ, "as propitiation by His blood." The Trinity is assumed in the work accomplished in redemption and propitiation. D. Martyn Lloyd-Jones writes, "What the Apostle teaches here [i.e., in Romans 3:25] is that what our Lord did by his death upon the cross was to appease God's wrath. This is a statement to the effect that God's wrath has been appeased and that God has been placated as the result of the work our Lord did there by dying upon the cross."[17] To put it in Trinitarian terms: Paul is explaining that by his death upon the cross, God the Son appeased or satisfied the wrath of God the Father.

The sacrificial nature of propitiation is seen in the phrase "by His blood," i.e., by Christ's blood. The mention of blood points the reader to the cross of Christ. Christ offers his blood, that is, his life, on the cross. Therefore, when Christ sheds his blood on the cross, that same blood is the means whereby the Father's wrath for sin and toward sinners is satisfied. Propitiation for sin is achieved by Christ's blood shed on the cross.

---

17. Lloyd-Jones, *Romans*, 70.

Part II: Redemption Accomplished

The propitiation accomplished by Christ on the cross is effectively applied "through faith" (LSB).[18] Without faith, there is no propitiation. Faith has been stressed thus far in Romans (1:16–17; 3:22) and will continue to be in view (3:26, 28). It is faith "in Jesus Christ" (v.22) and "in Jesus" (v.26). Hence, faith delimits propitiation to the faithful. The removal of sin and the appeasement of God's wrath is only effective for those with faith in Christ Jesus.

1 John 2:1–2

> My little children, I am writing these things to you so that you may not sin. But if anyone does sin, we have an advocate with the Father, Jesus Christ the righteous. He is the propitiation for our sins, and not for ours only but also for the sins of the whole world. (1 John 2:1–2)

The Trinitarian emphasis on the atonement is seen yet again as it is the Son—Jesus Christ the righteous one—who is the Christian's advocate with the Father. The Son does not plead our innocence since we are sinners (cf. 1:8, 10). We have sin. We have sinned. We sin. This is why we need an advocate who does not plead our case (we don't have one); rather, he acknowledges our guilt and presents his own completed work in our place as the grounds for our acquittal.

The question which must be answered based on this text is, "What does it mean for Jesus to be 'the propitiation for our sins'?" Then, attention must also be given to the question, "What does it mean for Jesus to be propitiation 'for the sins of the whole world'?"

The answer to both of these questions is rooted in the nature of the atonement and the context of the passage, both the immediate context and the wider context. Most read this verse and assume it says Jesus died for everyone. The challenge of laying aside what we *think* the text says so that what the text *actually* says remains. The immediate and larger context, in addition to the nature of the atonement (propitiation), undercuts the view that this text says Jesus died for each and every person.

First, John says that Christ is propitiation "for our sins." The "our" here is significant and immediately delimits the extent of Christ's propitiatory sacrifice to the Christians to whom John writes and includes John himself.

---

18. The ESV's "to be received by faith" is a bit too free in translation, inserting the phrase "to be received." The LSB's "through faith" is a better rendering of *dia pisteōs*.

Propitiation

In this phrase, John is drawing a sharp line of demarcation between the saints of God whose sins are propitiated for in Jesus Christ and all other people who remain in their sins, including the gnostic heretics who were threatening the church. Christ is not propitiation for their sins.

Second, John says that Christ is propitiation "not for ours only, but also for the sins of the whole world." A surface reading would read the phrase "the whole world" as "each and every person ever." Thus, "the sins of the whole world" means "the sins of each and every person who has ever lived." Jesus, then, is propitiation for the sins of each and every person ever. However, if "the sins of the whole world" means "the sins of each and every person ever," then no one would experience the wrath of God since Jesus is the sacrifice that satisfies God's wrath for the sins of each and every person ever. If God's wrath for sin is satisfied, then no wrath remains. The sins of Pharaoh, the Amorite high priest, and Judas are propitiated by Christ. Even the sins of the Gnostic heretics, the very sins they deny even sinning, are satisfied by the sacrifice of Christ. No one—not Pharaoh, the Amorite high priest, Judas, or the gnostic heretics—faces God's wrath for their sins if Jesus is propitiation for the sins of each and every person ever.

Someone might respond that Jesus' sacrifice provides the *possibility* of propitiation. His atoning sacrifice opens a gate whereby anyone can walk through if they have faith. Such a response does not square with what John wrote though. John does not present the atonement of Christ as hypothetical or potential but as actual. Christ Jesus *is* propitiation. The verb "is" in the phrase "He is the propitiation" is in the indicative mood, which is the mood of reality. Hence, Jesus himself is propitiation, i.e., his sacrifice on the cross in reality/actuality satisfies the wrath of God, "for the sins of the whole world." However, if that is the case, John contradicts John since it is John who says God's wrath abides on the disobedient (John 3:36). In addition, John envisions the final outpouring of God's wrath upon sin in the second death, the lake of fire (Rev 20:15). Scripture is clear that in the here and now, and in the there and then, unbelievers suffer the wrath of God for sins. But the wrath of God cannot exist, now or at the end, if Jesus is propitiation for the sins of each and every person since that would mean the punishment for their sins (wrath) has been satisfied, turned away, removed in Christ Jesus. Thus, the meaning of the words and phrases necessitates delimitation of the phrase "for the sins of the whole world."

Assuming "the sins of the whole world" means "the sins of each and every person ever" would also require universalism, i.e., the salvation of each

Part II: Redemption Accomplished

and every person. But such a view is foreign to Scripture. There are saved people, and there are unsaved people. Many unsaved people die in that state. Therefore, every view which seeks to maintain consistency with the entire biblical witness must delimit the phrase "the whole world" lest they end up with the heresy of universalism. So then, what does John mean when he writes that Jesus himself is propitiation for the sins of the whole world?

As has been argued elsewhere, there is a connection between John's gospel and his epistle. The epistle is intended to clarify and condemn distortions produced by the errant reading of the gospel by what appear to be proto-gnostics. Therefore, there are strong allusions to words and phrases found in John's gospel. The entire verse 2 is another example of such an echo. In John 11:51–52, John offers an interpretation of the high priest Caiaphas's announcement that it is better "that one man should die for the people, not that the whole nation should perish." John writes that Caiaphas was an unwitting prophet, God overruling his proclamation, so that "he prophesied that Jesus would die for the nation, and not for the nation only, but also to gather into one the children of God who are scattered abroad." Notice the parallel construction: Jesus' death for a specific people, and not for that specific people only but for a larger group. Such construction seems intentional: "for our sins" corresponds to "for the nation," i.e., the believing Jewish remnant. But while Christ's sacrifice is for the Jew first, it is not for the sins of the Jewish remnant only. "The children of God who are scattered abroad" corresponds to "the sins of the whole world," i.e., believing gentiles.

That propitiation is specific to Christians is also clear by the substitutionary nature of the atonement: "for our sins . . . for the sins, etc." With the satisfaction of the penalty for sin (wrath) comes the change in how the holy God deals with us on account of Christ. Christians are no longer under the wrath of God; now we have eternal life (cf. John 3:36). In addition, the contextual argument which is aimed squarely at the proto-gnostic heretics further delimits the meaning of the phrase "the sins of the whole world" to Christians. The proto-gnostic heretics were the ones claiming "we have no sin" and "we have not sinned" (1 John 1:8, 10). John counters these claims by calling them what they are: self-deception and lies. Then, in 2:1–2, he counters the proto-gnostic claims by affirming the need for things the heretics would not need: an advocate for when we sin and propitiation. Why would the sinless proto-gnostic heretics need an advocate since they do not sin? Is Jesus propitiation for the sins of the proto-gnostic heretics who deny they have sin? How could he be? They claim to have no sin, which needs to be propitiated. Thus, since Jesus is not propitiation for these individuals, "the whole world" cannot mean "each and every person ever."

Furthermore, the nature of the atonement concerning its permanence also factors into the interpretation. Jesus himself "is" propitiation (present tense). So it may be that "for our sins" may capture the living believers when John wrote this epistle. But the ingathering of God's children "who are scattered abroad" (perfect tense, were and continue to be scattered) in "the whole world" continues. There are other children of God, throughout all ages and in various places throughout "the whole world" that Christ continues "to gather into one"; as they come to faith in Christ, their sins are propitiated.

All of these delimiting factors lead one to recognize that when John says Jesus himself is propitiation for the sins of the whole world, he means that Jesus' sacrifice (viz., blood, 1:7) satisfies God's wrath for the sins of all believers from all nations, ethnicities, times, places, and conditions.

1 John 4:9–10

> In this the love of God was made manifest among us, that God sent his only Son into the world, so that we might live through him. In this is love, not that we have loved God but that he loved us and sent his Son to be the propitiation for our sins. (1 John 4:9–10)

God's love is always primary. "He loved us." As seen in John 17:23, those given to the Son by the Father are loved by the Father "even as You love Me," says Jesus. Jesus goes on to say that the Father loved him "before the foundation of the world" (v. 24). So as the Father loved the Son from eternity, so too the Father has loved those he has given to the Son from eternity.

This is because God is love. Since God is "from everlasting to everlasting" so his love is "an everlasting love" (Ps 90:2; Jer 31:3). God is the ultimate source of all love, including our love for him. Thus, God's love for us necessarily precedes our love for him. It is God's love which further militates against God being arbitrary. An ultimate being who acts according to his eternal love cannot be arbitrary.

Indeed, John affirms that we did not love God. Prior to conversion, we were weak, ungodly, sinners, who were enemies of God with darkened foolish minds that were hostile to God (Rom 5:6–8; 8:7). Yet, when we were unlovable, God loved us and sent his Son into the world to be propitiation for our sins.

In love and before the foundation of the world, God predestined us for adoption (Eph 1:4–5). That God loves us from eternity is a biblical fact (John 17:23b-24). Why he should love us is not the result of anything in us; the reason for God's love for us is found exclusively in him. The revelation of his love in history in the atonement (the Father sends the Son as propitiation for our sins) is an act of grace and the accomplishment of the divine intention. Therefore, God is glorified in the Son satisfying the wrath of God for the sins of his people on the cross.

The Trinitarian nature in propitiation is seen in verse 10. John says God sends his Son to be propitiation. We can say that God sends God as the sacrifice which satisfies God's wrath for our sins. The Father, for his love for us, sends his Son to be the propitiation for our sins.

Once again, the specificity of propitiation is seen in the phrase "for our sins." John once more includes himself with those to whom he is writing as those whose sins have been removed. This can be extended to all the believers who read what John has written. Indeed, every Christian can affirm that Christ is propitiation for their sins. Their sins have been removed by the Son so that they can have fellowship with the Father who has loved them from eternity.

Hebrews 2:17

> Therefore he had to be made like his brothers in every respect, so that he might become a merciful and faithful high priest in the service of God, to make propitiation for the sins of the people. (Heb 2:17)

"Therefore" connects what is to come with what came before. In order to help the seed of Abraham (v. 16), deliver those subject to lifelong slavery (v. 15), and through death destroy death and the devil (v. 14), it was necessary for Christ to be made like his brothers.

It was essential for God the Son to take on human form. "He had to be made like His brothers" shows the necessity of the incarnation. Without Christ sharing in flesh and blood, he is unable to help "the seed of Abraham." Without Christ taking on human nature, atonement could not be made. Without Christ taking on flesh, he could not be "a merciful and faithful high priest." Christ being "made like His brothers" was indispensably necessary.[19] There was no other way to accomplish redemption.

Christ was fully human and shares in humanity in all respects except one: sin. God the Son was "made like his brothers in every respect" yet without sin (cf. 4:15b). He had a real body of flesh and a soul or spirit. He had everything essential to human nature. But he was free from sin, "holy, innocent, unstained, separate from sinners" (7:26). This shows that sin is not essential to human nature.

Further, it is by the Son's taking on human nature that he is able to be high priest. As a high priest "like His brothers" he is able to sympathize with us, having been tempted "in every respect" as we are (4:15). According to his human nature, he is a "merciful" high priest. God in himself is merciful, has mercy, and "He has mercy on whomever He wills" (Rom 9:18). The mercy God the Son has as God in himself is further accentuated as the Spirit produces mercy in Christ and as his heart is moved with pity and sorrow for sinners. According to his human nature, he is a "faithful" high priest. God is faithful in himself, "abounding . . . in faithfulness" (Exod 34:7). God the Son offers faithful obedience to his Father through the Spirit in discharging his priestly duties in both offering as priest and being offered as the sacrifice. Whereas we lack the requisite faithfulness to give God what God desires and commands, God the Son has given God the faithfulness God requires. The Son accomplished the work the Father set before him (John 17:4). Also, he is faithful toward us, not only in being the author or originator of our salvation, but also in being the finisher of our faith in bringing us to glory (Heb 2:10).

Christ as high priest made propitiation for the sins of the people. This phrase brings into view all aspects of the nature of propitiation, either directly or indirectly. The offense (sins) is in view. So too are the ones offending (the people). Christ Jesus, specifically his death on the cross, is the sacrifice offered which satisfies God's wrath for the sins of the people. Implied in the statement is God who is offended by the sins of the people and whose wrath must be turned away from the people lest they be consumed (cf. 12:29). Christ as high priest offers himself to God through the Spirit to turn away God's wrath by taking away the people's sins. The four essential elements of propitiation identified by Owen are here represented.

---

19. Louw and Nida provide the definition as "to be necessary or indispensable" (*Greek-English Lexicon*, 671).

Part II: Redemption Accomplished

The object of Christ's propitiation, i.e., those needing propitiation due to sin, are "the people." Contextually, "the people" are those given by the Father to the Son (v. 13) who are also called Christ's "brothers" (v. 11, 12, 17) and "sons" whom Christ is bringing to glory (v. 10). They are the seed of Abraham that Christ helps (v. 16). Some commentators argue that this is "the people of Israel," i.e., Jewish Christians. However, Abraham was promised that his seed would be more numerous that the dust of the earth, the sands of the seashore, and the stars in the heaven.[20] In addition, Abraham was promised that in his seed "all families of the earth" and "all nations of the earth shall be blessed."[21] The international scope of the blessing widens the application of it beyond the borders of Israel and beyond the Jewish people. People from "all nations" are incorporated into the blessing of Abraham through the seed of Abraham who achieved the blessing, viz. Christ. In Christ, the promise made to Abraham of international blessing is fulfilled through the gospel.

This aligns with what Paul says in Galatians. On the one hand, Paul specifically identifies Christ as the seed of Abraham through whom the promise is fulfilled (Gal 3:16). On the other hand, Paul says in Christ the international blessing of Abraham has come to the gentiles so that those who are Christ's are Abraham's seed, "heirs according to promise" (Gal 3:14, 29). In Christ, people from all nations and families on the earth are by faith the seed of Abraham. Therefore, the identity of Christ's people carries international significance, inclusive of both Jews and gentiles.

Further, the use of the definite article with both "sins" and "people" serves to specify the locus of the work of Christ in atonement: *the* sins of *the* people. Only the sins of the people of Christ are propitiated by the high priest. The wrath of God due "the sins of the people" has been satisfied and turned away through the sacrifice of Christ. All people who are not Christ's remain under their sins, which means they remain under the wrath of God for their sins. Here is definite atonement.

What God the Son did on the cross through God the Holy Spirit was to offer himself to God the Father as the ransom price for sinners (cf. Heb 9:14–15). This did not produce a mere hypothetical or potential salvation;

---

20. While reiterated to all the patriarchs, the promise is specifically spoken to Abraham in Gen 12:2 ("a great nation"); 13:6 ("dust of the earth"); 17:4, 6; 18:18; 22:17 ("stars of the heaven and as the sand that is on the seashore").

21. While reiterated to all the patriarchs, the promise is specifically spoken to Abraham in Gen 12:3 ("all families of the earth shall be blessed"); 18:18 ("all nations of the earth"); 22:18 ("all nations of the earth").

it did not make people saveable. The sacrifice of the Son through the Spirit to the Father really did accomplish propitiation. The triune God was in Christ on the cross actually saving people.

All those given by the Father to the Son died with him; we were, each one, crucified with him (Gal 2:20; cf. Col 2:20). God the Son in the person of Jesus the Christ died for us, in our place, and on our behalf. He died the death due us. He took upon himself, in his person and body, the wrath of the Father for our sins. Since all the wrath of God almighty for our sins has been exhausted in the Son on the cross, the believer no longer abides under God's wrath but has eternal life.

Part III

Redemption Applied

Thus far it has been demonstrated that the triune God has been active in redemption from eternity. In eternity, the Father takes the lead in election, predestination, and the giving of a particular people to the Son for whom he will die. Then, in history, the Son takes the lead in taking on flesh to live sinlessly, die on the cross in union with all his people, atone for their sins, and turn away the wrath of the Father.

Now we take another step forward in history to the moments when God the Holy Spirit takes the lead in perfectly applying the completed work of Christ to his people, granting life, faith, and repentance to the glory of God the Father. It is the Holy Spirit who takes the lead in converting sinners and applying redemption to them. But, as seen each step of the way, this is not work done in isolation. In the perfect application of redemption the entire triune God is working harmoniously to accomplish their glorious purposes.

God sends God into our hearts. God the Holy Spirit is the person within the Trinity who takes the lead in the application of the completed work of Christ to people throughout time. That is, the Holy Spirit is the agent through whom the glorious purpose of the Father's election and the finished work of the Son's atonement is realized in time and space in the objects of redemption, namely, those given by the Father to the Son in eternity and for whom the Son dies on the cross in history.

Chapter 8

The Spirit Gives Life

The Spirit is the life-giver. Jesus says, "It is the Spirit who gives life" (John 6:63). Paul says, "The Spirit gives life" (2 Cor 3:6). Paul also says, "The Spirit is life" (Rom 8:10). Indeed, the Holy Spirit is "the Spirit of the living God" and "the Spirit of life" (2 Cor 3:3; Rom 8:2). This is due, in part, to the lordship of the Holy Spirit. The lordship of the Spirit is taught by Paul: "The Lord is the Spirit" (2 Cor 3:17). As Lord, the Spirit is sovereign over life, sustaining and maintaining this creation. Psalm 104 exalts the glorious work of Yahweh in the midst of his creation—sustaining, upholding, providing, and taking away. The Spirit's role is seen in verse 30: "When you send forth your Spirit, they are created, and you renew the face of the ground" (Ps 104:30). The creative and renewing work of the Spirit generally is highlighted in this text. The work of the Trinity in creation is a glorious whole and single work: the Father providing, the Son holding together, the Spirit sustaining. The Lord, even the Spirit, provides blessings generally for all people—the righteous and the unrighteous—as he pleases and to his glory. The general blessings of this life which are common to all people have historically been called "common grace."

Since the Spirit is the Lord of life, he must be by necessity the giver of life (cf. John 6:63). This is true not only with physical life but also with spiritual life. The Spirit works to grant new life to dead sinners. Without this work, there can be no new life. And it is entirely the Spirit's work, the power of God at work to bring new spiritual life. People cannot regenerate themselves. Humans do not have the power to raise themselves from spiritual death to spiritual life. Thus, it is God the Holy Spirit who powerfully works to regenerate dead sinners, granting new spiritual life.

The work of the Spirit in regeneration is not isolated from the work of the Father and the Son. Indeed, Jesus affirms that the triune God is united in giving life. First, the Son affirms that he does "nothing of His Own accord" (John 5:19), lit. from himself (*aph heautou*). As seen elsewhere in this work,[1] that is a phrase which denotes that no one person of the Godhead operates without reference to the other two persons. Neither the Son nor the Spirit will give life independent of the divine will. Jesus strengthens this by adding, "For whatever the Father does, that the Son does likewise" (5:19b). The Father, the Son, and the Holy Spirit (cf. John 16:13) neither do nor say anything independent of one another. There is glorious harmony within the Godhead.

This principle is then applied to the work of regeneration. Jesus says, "For as the Father raises the dead and gives them life, so also the Son gives life to whom he will" (John 5:21). The triune God works harmoniously to grant life. The Father, the Son, and the Holy Spirit all give life. Moreover, those who receive this life receive it according to the sovereign will of the triune God. "The Son gives life to whom He will," says Jesus. It has already been established that the Son does nothing "from Himself." Neither does the Spirit do anything "from Himself." Hence, the giving of life by the triune God is according to a single divine will. The Son and the Spirit do what the Father does. Thus, the triune God is united in granting life to whom they will.

All of this is vital to a proper understanding of the work of the Holy Spirit in regeneration. While the entire triune God, being the very source of life, gives life, it is the Holy Spirit who takes the lead in sovereignly giving life to those chosen by the Father and redeemed by the Son. According to the divine will, those chosen by the Father and redeemed by the Son are then, at the proper time, regenerated by the Holy Spirit. Indeed, as it pleased the Son to perfectly accomplish the redemption of those given to him by the Father, so it pleases the Holy Spirit to perfectly apply the completed work of Christ to all those given him by his Father. The good, pleasing, and perfect will of the Spirit is completely at one with that of the Father and the Son.

---

1. See chapter 2, "Harmony Between the Father, the Son, and the Holy Spirit."

The Spirit Gives Life

ALEXANDER CAMPBELL AND PRETERNATURAL HUMANITY

Sadly, most members of the churches of Christ do not recognize the sound of the voice of their own pioneer. While Alexander Campbell shook off many of the vestiges of his Scottish Presbyterianism, a clean break was not possible. Campbell's book *The Christian System* offers succinctly his doctrine of humanity. After citing Eccl 7:29, he remarks that "the natural man," which for Campbell is Adam, "became preternatural," a word that ought to cause us some confusion since it is (a) not found in the Bible, and (b) is used by Campbell in a specific manner. "Preternatural" for Campbell is his way of describing fallen humanity. In his debate with Nathan Rice, a Presbyterian, Campbell argued, "But man has strayed away from God and nature, and has become a preternatural being."[2] This occurred in Adam, the "fountain" whereby "the stream of humanity" has been "contaminated."[3] What Campbell means by "preternatural" is "we all inherit a frail constitution, physically, intellectually, but especially morally frail and imbecile."[4] He then cites Gen 5:3 ("Adam . . . fathered a son in his own likeness"), a common text utilized historically to teach the hereditary nature of the fall. Campbell mistakenly applies this text to Cain rather than Seth. Nevertheless, Campbell's point is clear: "We have all inherited our father's [Adam's] constitution and fortune."[5]

It is also helpful to situate Campbell's understanding of the fall within the larger framework of his anthropology. According to Campbell's doctrine of humanity, there are three stages. First, Adam was created a "natural" man. Then he sinned and became a "preternatural" man. This preternatural constitution is the present state of humans. In Christ we hope to be elevated to "supernatural" men.[6] Campbell thus argues in his debate with Rice, using 1 Cor 2:14 as his text.

It should be plainly obvious that this tripartite reading of Paul is foreign to the text. Indeed, Paul only argues for two states of humanity. Moreover, Paul's comments concern contemporary humanity and in no way represent an historical view. For Paul, there is "the natural person" and

---

2. Gould, *Debate*, 710.
3. Campbell, *Christian System*, 28.
4. Campbell, *Christian System*, 28.
5. Campbell, *Christian System*, 28.
6. Gould, *Debate*, 709.

Part III: Redemption Applied

"the spiritual person." He writes, "The natural person does not accept the things of the Spirit of God, for they are folly to him, and he is not able to understand them because they are spiritually discerned" (1 Cor 2:14). So Campbell attempts to interpret "natural" as "animal," which is akin to "preternatural."[7] Then, following this uncanny interpretation, Campbell turns around and protests concerning "the nomenclature of modern theology." He doth protest too much! Indeed, he borders on incoherence since he is protesting his own invention of categories foreign to Scripture.

Despite his poor reading of 1 Cor 2:14, a reading Rice pounced on during the debate,[8] Campbell's understanding of "preternatural" or fallen humanity is something forgotten to the mists of history by many in the churches of Christ. Because we are not aware of Campbell's lingering Presbyterian doctrine of humanity, many members object to what turns out to be a biblical anthropology. For example, read carefully this section from Campbell's chapter "Man as He Is":

> *In Adam, all have sinned*; therefore "in Adam all die." Your nature, gentle reader, not your person, was in Adam when he put forth his hand to break the precept of Jehovah. You did not personally sin in that act; *but your nature then in the person of your father, sinned against the Author of your existence.* In the just judgment, therefore, of your heavenly Father, *your nature sinned in Adam*, and with him it is right, that all human beings should be born *mortal*, and that death should lord it over the whole race as he has done in innumerable instances even "over them that have not sinned after the similitude of Adam's transgression;" i. e., by violating a positive law. Now it must be conceded, that what God can righteously and mercifully inflict upon a part of mankind, he may justly and mercifully inflict upon all; and therefore those that live one score or four score years on this earth, *for the sin of their nature in Adam*, might have been extinguished the first year as reasonably as those who have in perfect infancy perished from the earth. Death is expressly denominated by an Apostle, "*the wages of sin.*" Now this reward of sin is at present inflicted upon at least *one fourth* of the human race who have never violated any law, or sinned personally by any act of their lives. According to the most accurate bills of mortality, from one third to one fourth of the whole progeny of man die in infancy, under two years, without the consciousness of good or evil. They are thus, innocent though they be, as respects

---

7. Gould, *Debate*, 709–10.
8. Gould, *Debate*, 714–15.

actual and personal transgression, accounted as sinners by him who inflicts upon them the peculiar and appropriate wages of sin. This alarming and most strangely pregnant of all the facts in human history, proves that Adam was not only the common father, but *the actual representative of all his children.*[9]

First, "gentle reader," have you ever read this paragraph from Campbell before? I grew up in the churches of Christ and can say that not only had I never read it, but had it been read to me, and if I did not know it was from Campbell, I probably would have called it "Calvinistic." Second, for Campbell, what it means for humans to be "preternatural" is their "nature sinned in Adam . . . the actual representative of all his children." Now all of Adam's children are subject to death, including infants. This was Campbell's accounting for the death of 25 percent of humans in infancy, a staggering contemporary statistic. Campbell was well-aware that one cannot have an effect without a cause. Therefore, the effect of death is visited upon infants due to the sin of Adam, which thereby corrupted their nature (cause).

Third, "In Adam, all have sinned; therefore 'in Adam all die'" is derived from Rom 5:12: "so death spread to all men because all sinned." Sin came in via "one man," Adam, followed closely by Death, both of which exercise a tyrannical reign together (v. 14, 17, 21). Sin and Death are personified forces which exercise dominion over all human beings. Campbell traced the beginning of their tyrannical reign back to Adam. Adam was "the actual representative of all his children."

Fourth, Campbell distinguished between actual sin and original sin. People are not guilty of "actual and personal transgression" until they violate God's law. However, every human is born into the world carrying Adam's debt inasmuch as he was their representative at the beginning. Hence, even infants are "accounted as sinners" by God, which explains infant mortality for Campbell.

DEAD IN SIN

Why is it that the Spirit must grant new life if a soul will be saved? The Spirit's granting of life is emphasized because of the deadness of humanity in sin. Humankind is dead in trespasses and sin (Eph 2:1, 5; Col 2:13). Overwhelmingly the Scriptures affirm this basic truth. "Dead in sin" is the

---

9. Campbell, *Christian System*, 28–29. Emphasis for "mortal," "the wages of sin," and "one fourth" original; other emphases mine.

anthropological starting point for any discussion of the Spirit's work in the hearts of people. Jesus spoke of "the dead [who] bury their own dead," the former being those who are spiritually dead and the latter those who are physically dead (Matt 8:22). The father rejoices when the prodigal returns, acknowledging "this my son was dead" (Luke 15:24, 32). A self-indulgent widow "is dead even while she lives" (1 Tim 5:6). John says that one not loving his siblings "abides in death" (1 John 3:14). Clearly the Scriptures lean into the metaphor of death to describe sinners still in their sins.

Spiritual death has definite characteristics which are further elaborated throughout the Scriptures. Spiritual death impacts people's *minds*. Cognitively, unregenerate people are "futile in their thinking" (Rom 1:21) operating "in the futility of their minds" (Eph 4:17). "They are darkened in their understanding" (Eph 4:18). Hence, "No one understands" (Rom 3:11; cf. Ps 14:3). They are wise in their own eyes (Prov 26:12), but "claiming to be wise, they became fools" (Rom 1:22); indeed, "the wisdom of this world is folly with God" (1 Cor 3:19) so that God's assessment is, "Every man is stupid and without knowledge" (Jer 10:14). Each generation, then, inherits "futile ways" from their forefathers (1 Pet 1:18). It is because they are "corrupted in mind" (2 Tim 3:8) and out of their "debased mind" that they "do what ought not to be done" (Rom 1:28). They "oppose the truth" and "suppress the truth" in unrighteousness (2 Tim 3:8; Rom 1:18). They "despise wisdom and instruction" (Prov 1:7), "hate knowledge" (Prov 1:22), and "they are 'wise'—in doing evil!" (Jer 4:22).

Both testaments affirm that humans will devote their mental energies to imagining all manner of evil, especially gods and deities to replace the true God they have rejected. So the ignoble exchange has taken place whereby unregenerate humans "exchange the truth about God for a lie and worshiped and served the creature rather than the Creator" (Rom 1:25). Here is the impact spiritual death has upon the cognitive faculties of humans in all its grotesque deformity. The biblical data is sufficient to silence the philosophical rationalism inherent in Stone-Campbell Movement churches. Humans are cognitively fallen.

Spiritual death impacts people's *hearts*. The heart in Scripture is not only the seat of emotions; it is the center of a person. Heart (*kardia*), as Dunn points out, "had a broader use than its modern equivalent ("heart"), denoting the seat of the inner life . . . not only in reference to emotions, wishes and desires (e.g., [Rom] 1:24; 9:2), but also in reference to the will and decision making (e.g., 2 Cor 9:7) and to the faculty of thought and understanding," as Paul uses the term in Rom 1:21.[10] So the mind, the will, and the heart are closely linked.

Sin's effect upon the heart is presented throughout Scripture. "Their foolish hearts were darkened" points out the double blindness in humanity: first by the internal senselessness of the heart and second by the external darkness by which we are benighted. In fact, walking in darkness with blinded eyes is utilized repeatedly for unregenerate people (Acts 26:18; Rom 2:19; 1 John 2:11) The ignorance in unregenerate humanity is "due to their hardness of heart" (Eph 4:18). Indeed, their heart is "the heart of stone" (Ezek 11:19; 36:26), hearts that are "diamond-hard" (Zech 7:12), unwilling and unable to hear the Law of God and obey it. This is "an evil, unbelieving heart" (Heb 3:12). This problem is as old as time, since in Noah's day "every intention of the thoughts of [man's] heart was only evil continually" (Gen 6:5). Even after the flood "the intention of man's heart is evil from his youth" (Gen 8:21). People "are bent on turning away from" God (Hos 11:7). The wise man says, "The hearts of the children of man are full of evil, and madness is in their hearts while they live" (Eccl 9:3). The prophet Jeremiah says, "The heart is deceitful above all things and desperately sick" (Jer 17:9). Jesus himself says, "For from within, out of the heart of man . . . all these evil things come from" (Mark 7:21, 23). Human hearts are hardened, darkened, callous, foolish, evil, and unbelieving. Humans have a heart problem, and only God granting a new heart by his Spirit will remedy this heart condition.

Spiritual death impacts people's *affections*. It is from the stony, darkened, deceitful heart that disordered affections come. So one reads of people given over to "the lusts of their hearts to impurity, to the dishonoring of their bodies among themselves . . . dishonorable passions . . . that are contrary to nature" (Rom 1:26). People give themselves over to "sensuality, greedy to practice every kind of impurity . . . corrupt through deceitful desires" (Eph 4:22). Unregenerate people are "slaves to various passions and pleasures" (Titus 3:3). Jesus himself says, "People loved darkness rather than the light because their works were evil" (John 3:19). Paul also writes, "For people will be lovers of self, lovers of money, proud, arrogant, abusive, disobedient to their parents, ungrateful, unholy, heartless, unappeasable, slanderous, without self-control, brutal, not loving good, treacherous, reckless, swollen with conceit, lovers of pleasure rather than lovers of God" (2 Tim 3:2–4). Rather than loving God, they are "haters of God" who invent

---

10. Dunn, *Romans 1–8*, 60.

ways of doing evil (Rom 1:30). They are "hostile in mind" (Col 1:21), which means that since their minds are set on the flesh it is "hostile to God, for it does not submit to God's law; indeed, it cannot" (Rom 8:7). Thus, "No one seeks for God" (Rom 3:11). Rather than doing righteousness, "None is righteous, no, not one" (Rom 3:10; cf. Eccl 7:20). In fact, they have "pleasure in unrighteousness" (1 Thess 2:12). Instead of engaging in good works, "No one does good, not even one" (Rom 3:12; cf. Ps 14:3; 53:1; Eccl 7:20). This is why "all our righteous deeds are like a polluted garment" (Isa 64:6). Humans want what they want and therefore choose what they want. Unfortunately, because they love sin, they want the wrong things.

It is important to lay out explicitly what people deny implicitly. Most Christians want to blunt the force of the biblical doctrine of humanity. As we see, though, Scripture pulls no punches. Spiritual death impacts humans cognitively, morally, and volitionally. Their minds do not function properly. Their hearts love the wrong things. Their will is bent away from God. While the above biblical data is overwhelming, it is not exhaustive. Much more could be said. But what has been laid out is sufficient. The biblical anthropology is damning. We contribute only sin, trespass, guilt, and death to the situation.

There is a fundamental misunderstanding about what is meant by dead in sin. It is sometimes caricatured as though an unbeliever cannot understand the gospel. Or the unregenerate person is unable to respond to God. However, as White explains, "Unregenerate man is fully capable of understanding the facts of the gospel: he is simply incapable, due to his corruption and enmity, to submit himself to that gospel. And he surely responds to God every day: negatively, in rebellion and self-serving sinfulness."[11] An unbeliever can hear and know the facts of the gospel and can perhaps even assent to the reality of these facts. But because of the corruption of his mind, heart, and will, he refuses to trust God and rely upon Christ. Until God through the Spirit grants new spiritual life, the unbeliever will continue to rebel and refuse to submit to Christ as Lord.

Another fundamental misunderstanding about what is meant by dead in sin is that people are as evil as possible or that they always do evil. This is not what is meant. There are atheists who are philanthropists. Sinners do good things even before coming to Christ. Therefore, when Scripture speaks to humanity's deadness in sin, it does not mean humans *always* sin. Rather, due to the spiritual death within a person, all their person (mind,

---

11. White, *Potter's Freedom*, 101.

body, heart, will) is touched by sin and corrupted. Hence, the motivation behind those good deeds is not born from a spiritual desire for God or to express love for God. Good deeds are done for selfish reasons.[12] Or at best, regarding God, they do good deeds to get some benefit from God (e.g., "Since I'm basically a good person God will take me to heaven"). So an unbeliever can do good deeds, but because of their deadness in sin they do them for selfish or distorted reasons.

John Owen summarizes succinctly the anthropological starting point in contrast with God's essential character: "He is 'light, and in him is no darkness at all;' we are darkness, and in us there is no light at all. He is life, a 'living God;' we are dead, dead sinners,—dead in trespasses and sin. He is 'holiness,' and glorious in it; we wholly defiled,—an abominable thing. He is 'love;' we full of hatred,—hating and being hated."[13] God is light, life, and love. Unregenerate humans separated from Christ are darkness, death, and hatred.

---

12. In Matthew 6:1–18, Jesus gave three examples (alms, prayer, and fasting) of doing good for the wrong reason and defines them as hypocrisy.

13. Owen, *Works*, 2:107.

CHAPTER 9

The Spirit Gives Life to Those Given by the Father to the Son

ONE TEXT WHICH VIVIDLY demonstrates the regenerating work of the Spirit within the Trinitarian framework is John 6. John 6 begins with "a large crowd" enthralled with Jesus and ends with twelve bewildered followers, one of whom is a devil. At the beginning of the chapter, Jesus is so popular the crowds want to make him king by force (v. 15). At the end of the chapter, so many who were following him walk away that he asks the Twelve, "Are you going too?" What was it that sparked such a radical shift among the crowds that multitudes walked away? What was so unpopular in his teaching that Jesus offended so many? After feeding the five thousand (v. 1–15) and walking on water (v. 16–21), both impressive miracles which yet again confirm the true identity of God's Son, Jesus taught a lesson in a synagogue in Capernaum (v. 59). It is the content of this teaching that soured the crowds on Jesus so that "many of His disciples turned back and no longer walked with Him" (v. 66). What was the controversial teaching Jesus taught on this occasion? It was the truth of the human condition and the kingly freedom of the triune God.

The Spirit Gives Life to Those Given by the Father to the Son

CONTEXT (JOHN 6:1-34)

The day after Jesus feeds five thousand men and walks on the water, the crowds which had been fed and had desired to make Jesus king by force load up in boats and cross the sea to Capernaum "seeking Jesus" (John 6:22-24). However, their search is not an honest one; as Jesus will point out, they are only searching for him "because you ate your fill of the loaves" (v. 26). The crowds sought the benefits of Christ, not Christ himself. They are motivated by the flesh, not by faith. Indeed, it is their unbelief which Jesus is explaining in his discourse (v. 36). Jesus tells them that God requires "that you believe in Him whom He has sent" (v. 29). Trinitarian considerations are present in this statement since faith in the Son sent by the Father is what God, even the triune God, requires.

The crowd, no doubt mixed with both people who had been fed the previous day as well as townsfolk from Capernaum, ask for a sign "that we may see and believe you" (v. 30). The question assumes their own unbelief. Further, the emphasis is on sight—"see and believe"—which betrays a faulty understanding of faith. Jesus will go on to affirm they have seen him, which even included miracles, "yet do not believe" (v. 36). These crowds are unbelievers who are bent on satisfying their material needs, viz., filling their bellies. This is further evidenced by their appeal to Moses and the manna (v. 31).

Jesus clarifies that it was not Moses but his Father who gives them the bread from heaven (v. 32). A conversation about bread is not accidental; the context of those discussion is the Passover when the Jewish people ate unleavened bread (v. 4). What is significant is the origin, nature, and aim of this "bread from heaven." First, "my Father gives you the true bread from heaven" (v. 32). It is from the Father, the Father's gift "from heaven." The Father is the source of this bread. He is the only one who can give it. This point is stressed here because other things in this context are given by God and can only be given by him (v. 37, 39, 65). Second, Jesus clarifies "the bread of God is He who comes down from heaven," going even further by saying, "I am the bread of life" (v. 33, 35). The nature of this bread is not physical but spiritual; it is not food but a person. Third, "the bread of God . . . gives life to the world" (v. 33). Although it is given to "you," i.e., the Jews (cf. 1:11), the Father's gift gives life to "the world," i.e., believers from all over the world, Jews and gentiles. No wonder those who heard him said, "Sir, give us this bread always" (v. 34).

Part III: Redemption Applied

This is the context for Jesus' teaching in verses 35ff. Without this contextual framework, any exegetical work will collapse on itself. God the Son is addressing a crowd of unbelievers concerning their unbelief. He explains why some believe and some do not. If anyone would know and can reveal the cause of their unbelief, indeed any person's unbelief, it is the second person of the Godhead.

ALL GIVEN BY THE FATHER TO THE SON COME TO THE SON

In verses 35ff, Jesus makes several statements concerning the will of the Father and the Son's accomplishment of the Father's will. These theological statements are often overshadowed by prior philosophical considerations concerning human will. The priority in the text, though, is not human will but the triune God's will.

> Jesus said to them, "I am the bread of life. He who comes to Me will never hunger, and he who believes in Me will never thirst." (John 6:35, LSB)

As established, Jesus is addressing unbelievers concerning their unbelief. Though they cry out for Jesus to "give us this bread always," they desire the benefits Jesus can give them, not Jesus himself. Jesus begins with a self-revelation: "I am the bread of life." The very thing they claim to want, the bread from heaven, is standing before them, but they do not want him. Indeed, by the end of the discourse many will turn back and cease following him (v. 66).

Next, Jesus makes a statement about coming to him. The LSB does well in translating the present participles. Hence, "he who comes . . . he who believes," or even the one coming and the one believing. The parallel of coming and believing is evident. Ryle writes:

> The words 'coming' and 'believing' in this sentence appear to mean very nearly one and the same thing. To 'come' to Christ is to 'believe' on Him, and to 'believe' on Him is to 'come' to Him—both expressions mean that act of the soul whereby, under a sense of its sins and necessity, it applies to Christ, casts itself on Christ.— 'Coming' is the soul's movement towards Christ. 'Believing,' is the soul's venture on Christ.—If there is any difference, it is that 'coming' is the first act of the soul when it is taught by the Holy Ghost, and that 'believing' is a continued act or habit which never ends.

The Spirit Gives Life to Those Given by the Father to the Son

> No man 'comes' who does not believe; and all who come go on believing.[1]

Coming to Jesus is paralleled with belief/faith in Jesus. Connected with this, and also vital to proper understanding of the discourse, are the metaphors of eating and drinking. The one coming to and believing in Jesus "will never go hungry . . . will never be thirsty." This sheds light on Jesus' later statements about eating his flesh and drinking his blood; these are not statements about the Lord's Supper or the Eucharist but about faith in him.

Those who were hearing Jesus, though, were not believers, as Jesus himself points out (v. 36). Why did they not believe? It is because coming to and believing in the Son is predicated upon having been given by the Father to the Son. Only those who belong to the triune God will continue coming to and believing in the Son.

This is in perfect agreement with other statements by Jesus later in John's gospel. Jesus tells the Jews, "Whoever is of God hears the words of God. The reason why you do not hear them is that you are not of God" (8:47). To be "of God" means belonging to God the Father and has been born of God, i.e., to be his children. To "hear the words of God" means to hear the words and receive them. So the reason why the Jews who Jesus was speaking to did not hear so as to receive the words of the Son is because they were not of the Father. Then, on another occasion Jesus tells the Jews, "You do not believe because you are not among [lit. of] My sheep" (10:26). To be "of My sheep" means to belong to the flock of the good Shepherd, i.e., Jesus. Hence, the reason those to whom Jesus was speaking did not believe in him was because they did not belong to him. Finally, when standing before Pilate, after he is asked, "So You are a King?" Jesus answered, "Everyone who is of the truth listens to My voice" (18:37). To be "of the truth" means to belong not merely to that which corresponds to reality but to him who is, was, and ever will be the Truth. So the one who belongs to the truth listens to Jesus.

In all three of the above instances, there is a temptation to reverse the order. How these verses are typically understood is that one belongs to the Father *because* they heard God's word; one belongs to the flock of the Shepherd *because* they believed; one belongs to the truth *because* they listened to Jesus. This is the direct opposite of what Jesus says, though. These did not hear *because* they did not belong to God; they did not believe *because* they did not belong the flock of the good Shepherd; Pilate did not listen to

---

1. Ryle, *Expository Thoughts*, 371.

Jesus *because* he did not belong to the truth, even the Truth, i.e., Jesus. Jesus' revelation of these truths provides us insight into the eternal decree of the triune God which is worked out in time. In time, what distinguishes those given by the Father to the Son (i.e., the elect) from those not given by the Father to the Son (i.e., the non-elect) is whether or not they are of God, of the shepherd's flock, and of the truth. It is the elect of God who in due time hear the words of God, receive it, come to the Son, and continue to believe in the Son. The non-elect do not and will not. This is the explanation by our Lord himself as to why the crowd did not believe.

> All that the Father gives me will come to me, and whoever comes to me I will never cast out. (John 6:37)

It is inescapable that certain people are given by the Father to the Son. It is not that they *give themselves* to Jesus; the Father gives them to the Son. This is so clearly taught by the Lord that it seems inexplicable that so many would miss this truth. Yet many do. I confess that for many years I did as well. I simply did not see the force of the truth that Jesus taught.

The present tense is used here in verse 37: the Father *gives* people to the Son. It is the Father's giving of these people to the Son which is the basis for their coming to Jesus. In other words, people come to Jesus because they are given by the Father to the Son. The use of the present tense verb—"gives"—signifies the historical outworking of the eternal will of God. The eternal work of the triune God is worked out in time and space, even in the present tense. Indeed, the present work of God is rooted in the counsel and purpose of the triune God from eternity (i.e., before time). Those given by the Father to the Son are given in the present because they have been given from eternity (cf. v. 39).

"All that" (*pan ho*) is neuter singular "depicting those whom the Father gave Jesus as a collective entity."[2] Lenski agrees that "all that" means "the whole mass of believers of all ages and speaks of them as a unit."[3] It is the whole lot of those who will come to and believe in Christ that is in view in the phrase. In addition, the coming, and therefore believing, of those given to the Son is presented not as a possibility but as a certainty. All those given by the Father to the Son "will come" to Jesus. "Will come" is in the indicative mood, the mood of reality, and so guarantees a particular people from among all fallen humanity coming to him. Faced with the unbelief

---

2. Kruse, *John*, 193.
3. Lenski, *St. John's Gospel*, 463.

The Spirit Gives Life to Those Given by the Father to the Son

and rebellion of those standing before him, Jesus affirms the goodness of his Father in giving him those who would believe in him and submit their lives to him.

The rest of Jesus' saying in this verse records the unbreakable chain from before all time to the end of time. Those given from eternity by the Father to the Son will in time come to Jesus, and he "will never cast" them out. The individual specificity whereby each and every one given by the Father to the Son is seen in the phrase "whoever comes" or, as it could be also be translated, "the one who comes to me." The present participle is used once again and can be translated "the one coming," also highlighting the continual nature of faith and the need to keep on coming to Jesus. It is "the one coming" that Jesus "will never cast out." And the reason they keep on coming to Jesus is because they are given by the Father to the Son. The triune God is presented as a perfect Savior since those given by the Father to the Son in eternity and individually come to Jesus in time will be saved eternally since Jesus will never cast out those given to him by the Father.

> For I have come down from heaven, not to do my own will but the will of him who sent me. (John 6:38)

Jesus' heavenly origin is clear from the phrase "I have come down from heaven." Just as "the bread of God is He who comes down from heaven," Jesus plainly affirms that he is that bread, and he has been sent by the Father. The Father resides in heaven, and he has sent his Son "from heaven." In condescending and assuming human nature to his divine person Jesus will faithfully fulfill the heavenly mission.

When Jesus says he came "not to do My Own will but the will of Him who sent Me," he is not pitting his will against the Father's will. Elsewhere in John's gospel Jesus affirms the opposite (4:34; 5:19; 17:4). The wills of the Father and the Son, while distinct, are united, aimed at the same end. The Father and the Son are in perfect harmony with one another. The Son delights in doing the Father's will, and the Father is glorified in the Son's obedience.

All of salvation is dependent upon the triune God's will: the Father's will in saving his elect, the Son's perfect obedience whereby he saves those given to him by the Father, and the Spirit's giving of life to dead sinners for whom Christ died. Accentuated here are the Father's will and the Son's obedience. Jesus' perfect obedience to the will of the Father is what ensures the salvation of those given to him. His obedience is counted to them as their obedience. In addition, Jesus perfectly obeying the Father in all things guarantees that the will of the triune God will be fully accomplished. Kruse highlights the impossibility of the triune God failing to accomplish his will:

> [The] eternal security [of those who believe] is tied to the Son's obedience to the Father, on the one hand, and to the will of the Father, on the other. For any of those whom the Father has given to his Son to be lost would mean that Jesus failed to carry out his Father's will and that the will of the Father had been thwarted. Both of these things are unthinkable.[4]

Jesus' words challenge the contemporary assertion made by some that God tries to save people but is thwarted time and again by the almighty will of humans. Such assertions betray a human-centered way of thinking which puts the human will above the divine will. Such thinking fails to recognize the force of Jesus' words. Further, such a thought—that the Son would fail to accomplish the Father's will in saving all those given to him—would result in the undoing of the Trinity since the Son fails to obey perfectly his Father's will. Finally, attempts to smuggle human will into this context must explain why the divine will is presented as the primary driving force behind faith, salvation, and resurrection (cf. v. 40, "the will of My Father"). The triune God will accomplish all his will perfectly.

> And this is the will of him who sent me, that I should lose nothing of all that he has given me, but raise it up on the last day. (John 6:39)

Once again it is immediately plain that there are those given by the Father to the Son. Jesus does not here give the timestamp for when the Father gave certain people to him. At the same time, it has already been established, based on the exegesis of John 17 elsewhere in this book, that the giving of people by the Father to the Son took place "before the foundation of the world" (John 17:24). Indeed, the same verb is used in the same tense there as here.[5] There is no reason to believe that Jesus here in John 6 would have a different reference point for when the Father gave certain people to him then he does in John 17 when he is praying to the Father.

---

4. Kruse, *John*, 194.

5. The verb *didōmi* is used in the perfect tense in John 6:39 as well as John 17:22, 24. The only difference is in 6:39 the verb is in the third person (*dedōken*, "He has given") while in 17:22, 24 it is in the second person (*dedōkas*, "You have given"). The reason for this is because the former is a public discourse to the Jews whereas the latter is private prayer to God.

The Spirit Gives Life to Those Given by the Father to the Son

Those chosen by the Father before the foundation of the world are given to the Son in eternity.

We have already seen from John 17 that it is out of love that the Father gives certain individuals from among the whole lot of fallen humanity to the Son for whom he will die. John 3:16 is a beloved passage of Scripture for many people; rightly so. It succinctly summarizes the gospel in a single verse. To borrow the phrasing and to incorporate the divine perspective Jesus presents here in John 6: God so loved the Son that he gave certain individuals from the whole lot of fallen humanity to the Son that he would die in their place on the cross for their sins to the glory of God.

The Father's will is that the Son be a perfect Savior. To accomplish this means the Son "shall lose none of all that he has given me," i.e., given to him by the Father (NIV). Losing even one person given to him by the Father would mean Christ is not a perfect Savior and therefore disobedient to his Father. Again, are we to suggest that the Son would fail in doing the Father's will? Such a failure would result in the undoing of the Godhead! Therefore, all those given to the Son by the Father will be saved and, on the last day, Christ will "raise them all up," i.e., raise them to eternal life (cf. 5:29).

Here is the security of the believer. Jesus states it two different ways, once negatively and once positively, to drive home the truth. First, of all those given him by the Father he shall lose none of them. Second, all those given him by the Father he will resurrect them to life at the end. It is humans, whose knowledge is imperfect and whose hearts are prone to doubts, that struggle with certainty and assurance of salvation. As Lenski points out, though, "In the mind of God, the giver, and of his Son, the receiver, no uncertainty ever existed about those who in all ages are made his own by grace through the gospel and by faith."[6] "The Lord knows those who are His" (2 Tim 2:19). It is faith, looking to Jesus, and coming to Christ that are the evidences of our election. By continued faith in the Son, by continually looking to Christ, and by continually coming to Jesus we find the assurance that we need that we belong to the triune God and he abides with us.

> For this is the will of my Father, that everyone who looks on the Son and believes in him should have eternal life, and I will raise him up on the last day. (John 6:40)

Once again the will of the Father is front and center. Jesus makes a plain assertion concerning what the divine will is: the ultimate salvation

---

6. Lenski, *St. John's Gospel*, 468.

("eternal life") of those who continue to trust in the Son. Prior to looking or beholding the Son and believing in him, these are all those given to the Son by the Father. So those given by the Father to the Son are those who keep on looking to and believing in the Son; these are also the same ones who will be raised up on the last day. There is, therefore, an unbroken chain from eternity to eternity which is the will of God.

There is a noteworthy shift from the corporate (group) view of election to the individual view of election in verses 39–40. Verse 39 emphasized the collective or corporate aspect of all those given to the Son by the Father ("raise *it* [*auto*] up on the last day"). Here in verse 40 the individual aspect of election is in view when Jesus says, "I will raise *him* [*auton*] up on the last day." This is further accentuated by the shift from the neuter "all" (*pan*) in verse 39 to the nominative masculine "everyone" (*pas*) here in verse 40 in conjunction with singular participles (therefore, "all the ones looking to the Son and believing in Him"). Thus, the false dichotomy some present between whether election is corporate or individual is unnecessary; both concepts are present in Scripture, even in the teaching of our Lord.

Then, there is the function of the subjunctive in this verse. It is well-known that the subjunctive mood is a mood of possibility and potentiality.[7] Generally speaking this is correct. However, syntactically when part of a clause introduced by a subordinating conjunction, the use of the subjunctive changes. For example, and with specific reference to the text before us, the subjunctive introduced in the clause by a *hina* indicates result-purpose. This involves "*both the intention and its sure accomplishment.*"[8] Wallace, citing BDAG, notes that such construction reflects theology where "purpose and result are identical in declarations of the divine will."[9] In other words, theology is reflected in this grammatical construction. This is precisely the point in Jesus' statement in verse 40 concerning the Father's will. God's will, both what he intends and what he accomplishes, is done.

A closer look at verse 40 shows that the phrase "should have eternal life" is contained within a clause introduced by a *hina*. The verb (*echē*) is a present subjunctive. The present tense indicates continuous action. Thus, "shall have eternal life" is a legitimate rendering. Coupled with the context this seems a more consistent rendering: it is "the ones beholding [present tense] the Son and the ones believing [present tense] in Him" who "shall

---

7. See for example Long, *Kairos*, 204.
8. See Wallace, *Greek Grammar*, 472–73. Emphasis original.
9. Wallace, *Greek Grammar*, 472.

have eternal life." Are we to conclude that one who is continually beholding the Son and continuing in loyalty to him might not have eternal life and be destroyed? Such a conclusion is contrary to what Jesus says. Hence, the promise of Christ raising such a one up at the resurrection (future indicative). Nothing will thwart God in accomplishing his intention for all those he has given to the Son.

Under discussion is the will of the Father accomplished by the Son on behalf of the ones given by the Father to the Son. Jesus came to do "the will of Him who sent Me" (v. 38). This indicates a singular divine intention, the Father and the Son willing the same thing. The will of the Father is that the Son "should lose [aorist subjunctive] nothing of all that He has given Me, but raise it up on the last day" (v. 39). Are we to assume it is possible that the Son may/might lose any of those given to him by the Father? Or as Murray asks, "Are we to entertain even the remotest suspicion that this will of the Father will be defeated?"[10] Indeed, it would be to the eternal shame of the Son to lose any of those given to him by his Father. Not to mention it would introduce disharmony into the divine will: the Father willing something that the Son fails to do. Rather, all the ones given by the Father to the Son will be raised up on the last day (v. 39b).

A STIR OF MURMURING (VS. 41–43)

In unbelief and rebellion, those who heard him speak of his divine origin rejected it. They clearly understood it; their question shows as much: "Is not this Jesus, the son of Joseph, whose father and mother we know?" They know Jesus is merely a carpenter's son, the son of Mary and Joseph. The crowds knew his parents, knew where he came from and that he is a local boy. "How does he now say, 'I have come from heaven'?" The contrast between their understanding and their unbelief is evident in their questions concerning Jesus natural origin contrasted with his teaching of his divine origin. As White observes, "It is not that they didn't understand what He was saying, but that they did not like what He was saying. Their words are soaked in unbelief and rebellion."[11] Though he is the son of Mary, he is also the Son of God. The crowds only recognize the former. They reject the latter. Indeed, they know his father on earth, but not his Father in heaven.

---

10. Murray, *Redemption Accomplished and Applied*, 168.
11. James White, *Drawn by the Father*, 67.

Part III: Redemption Applied

In the question which contains a quotation of Jesus' saying is the reason Jesus can provide the divine perspective on belief and unbelief. Jesus "came down from heaven." His origin is divine. He is the Son of God, even God the Son. He is the Lord of heaven and earth. Therefore, only he can provide the divine perspective as to why some believe and others do not. Their rejection of his divine origin is likewise a rejection of his divine teaching on the matter of divine sovereignty in faith and salvation.

It was true in Jesus' day; it is true today: people do not like a high view of the sovereignty of God. Jesus has come down from heaven in order to reveal and do the Father's will. However, the people "grumbled about Him." The Jews grumbling about Jesus is the same grumbling as the people in the wilderness at Yahweh.[12] Yahweh has come down from heaven, taken on flesh, and is dwelling among them in Jesus, but they refuse to believe. But they do not outright state their rejection, choosing to disguise their denial of Jesus with their seemingly pious questions. They ask questions to mask their unbelief.

Such a tactic does not work on the Lord. Jesus takes back control of the conversation from the murmurers (lit. the text says, "Jesus answered [*apekrithē*] and said"). Then, he exhorts them, "Stop grumbling with one another." The following teaching, aimed squarely at explaining the unbelief and murmuring of those who stood before him, is a solemn, sober revelation from heaven concerning the cause of both unbelief and faith.

DRAWN BY THE FATHER

> No one can come to me unless the Father who sent me draws him.
> And I will raise him up on the last day. (John 6:44)

The attempts to smuggle an autonomous or libertarian human will into this statement are myriad. For example, C. E. W. Dorris found David Lipscomb's comment on this text wanting. Lipscomb's entire comment is as follows: "None could come to Jesus unless taught and drawn by the Father."[13] Dorris

---

12. When the Hebrew Scriptures were translated into Greek, the word used to translate the people of Israel's grumbling in Exod 17:3 and Num 14:27, 29 is the same word used here by John of the Jews grumbling about Jesus. For example, in Exod 17:3 the Hebrew phrase (*wayyalen*) is translated with the Greek word *egonguzen* from *gonguzō*. The word "grumbled" in John 6:41 is *egonguzon*, which is from the same root.

13. Lipscomb, *John*, 99. Lipscomb wrote his comments in 1939. Dorris not only edited but provided additional comments for the 1956 edition.

thought Lipscomb too brief, and therefore in brackets he has supplemented with an accounting of two elements involved in coming to Christ: human will and divine drawing. Dorris then provides further commentary on the human side and divine side of coming to Christ, emphasizing the human ability to refuse to come to Christ. Writes Dorris, "If man's will consents, and he yields to the drawing power, he comes [to Christ]. If he 'will not,' and refuses to be drawn, he does not come. God will not force him. No one comes to Jesus unless he yields his own will and is drawn by the love of the Father manifested in the gospel."[14] Dorris's comments simply are eisegetical. Nowhere in Jesus' statement is there any discussion about people yielding their will. Further, Dorris's comments miss the plain meaning of the text. In fact, it shifts the focus from the will of God to the seemingly almighty human will.

Adam Clarke is another commentator who is determined to rescue human will from the clutches of divine sovereignty. He focuses his comments on the phrase "unless the Father ... draws him." He asks, "But how is a man drawn?" His answer cites Augustine who cites a poet, "[A] man is attracted by that which he delights in." Examples are taken from nature: sheep are drawn by green grass; children like nuts. Clarke concludes:

> They run wherever the person runs who shows these things: they run after him, but they are not forced to follow; they run, through the desire they feel to get the things they delight in. So God draws man: he shows him his wants—he shows the Saviour [sic] whom he has provided for him: the man feels himself a lost sinner; and, through the desire which he finds to escape hell, and get to heaven, he comes unto Christ, that he may be justified by his blood. Unless God thus draw, no man will ever come to Christ; because none could, without this drawing, ever feel the need of a Saviour [sic].[15]

So the drawing of the Father is "alluring" or "inciting," which, as Clarke notes, "The best Greek writers use the verb in the same sense."[16]

In response, first, it must be recognized that Clarke has glossed the first part of the verse: "No one can come to Me," says Jesus. Clarke assumes there are those who are able to "run after" God. In addition, because of sin humans are enemies of God, haters of God, rebel fugitives from God (Rom 5:10; 1:30; 3:11). "No one seeks for God," says Paul. Yet, Clarke has humans

---

14. Lipscomb, *John*, 99.
15. Clarke, *Clarke's Commentary*, 5:562.
16. Clarke, *Clarke's Commentary*, 5:562.

running after him! Such a claim runs contrary to the natural inclination of humans. In other words, there is nothing in unregenerate humans which would cause them to desire or delight in God. Second, while there may be other Greek writers who use the term "draws"[17] and perhaps in the way Clarke says, the question which must focus the exegete is "how does John use the word?" The word is used a half dozen times in the NT, five times by John (6:44; 12:32; 18:10; 21:6, 11). It is used of Peter drawing his sword from its sheath and dragging a net full of fish ashore. Are we to entertain the strange idea that Peter's sword ran out of his sheath because of the desire it felt to get the thing(s) it delighted in? Or that the net delighted in and desired to run ashore? Thus, due to Clarke's faulty anthropology and questionable word study, his exegesis is found lacking.

Burton Coffman is still another commentator, especially popular among Churches of Christ, who offers commentary on John 6:44. He questions the notion of "an irresistible and sovereign act of God in calling individual sinners" being found in this verse. He draws attention to the next verse which says, "They will all be taught by God" (v. 45). Coffman seems to universalize this text since he writes, "To suppose that God draws some and not others would be to suppose that God is partial and unjust."[18] In other words, the "all" who are "taught by God" are everyone everywhere since it would be partiality and injustice on God's part for certain people not to be taught.

In response several things must be considered. First, the context does not permit this reading by Coffman. It is the ones who are drawn by the Father who are also raised up on the last day (v. 44). If verse 45 and "they will all be taught by God" is universalized to include the whole scope of humanity, then every single human must come to Jesus too since the end of the verse says, "Everyone who has heard and learned from the Father comes to Me" [i.e., Jesus]. Hence, "all" in verse 45 must be delimited to all those drawn by the Father, who come to Jesus, and who will be raised up to eternal life—all of these are taught by the Father. Second, in connection to the preceding considerations, there is no injustice or partiality with God since those drawn by the Father to himself are just as much sinners deserving hell as the rest of humanity. There is nothing in those drawn by the Father which would cause them to merit God's grace. The charge of partiality or injustice is simply mistaken. Third, experience militates against Coffman's

---

17. Gk. *helkusē* from *helkuō*.
18. Coffman, "Commentary on John 6."

view since there have been people throughout church history who have never heard the gospel. More than that, if "all" in verse 45 must mean every single person ever, then it would have to include all those who lived before Jesus did. Such a universalized reading of "they will all be taught by God" does not fit the context, nor does it fit with reality.

Coffman is also one who champions the sovereign will of humans. He goes so far as to say that the murmurers were "thwarting God's drawing of them unto himself."[19] Witness the omnipotent will of these creatures! Behold, the impotence of the Father almighty! Such a statement by Coffman gives too much credit to these creatures. It also fails to recognize that Jesus is explaining their unbelief. It is not that they disbelieve because they were somehow thwarting God's drawing power. Rather, they are not drawn by the Father because they have not been given by the Father to the Son. Since they have not been given by the Father to the Son, they do not come to the Son nor do they believe in him.

A close reading of the text refutes Dorris's, Clarke's, Coffman's, and others' mistaken understanding of Jesus' words. First, we see the universal negative "no one." This means no human person and is all-inclusive. Second, Jesus addresses the question of ability with the term "can." However, contra Dorris and Clarke, no human will, in and of itself, is able to come to Jesus on its own. All humans are unable to yield their own wills to God's drawing power and come to Christ. People do not come to Christ of their own volition. They need divine enablement. Fortunately, the action of the Father is on the way. Third, we see a necessary condition which must be met before anyone is able to come to Jesus with the term "unless." The necessary condition is God the Father drawing a person ("him"). Once more, contra Dorris and Clarke, the word "draw" does mean "to compel" or even to "drag." As noted above, this is the same word used of the disciples' failed attempt to haul or drag the net full of fish to the boat (John 21:6). In addition, it is the word used by James to describe how the rich "drag" the poor saints into court (Jas 2:6). Similar usages could be added, but these suffice to show the compulsory nature of the term. Left to ourselves, we would never want Christ, let alone come to him.

In addition, lexical information further strengthens the case for the spiritual awakening taking place so that a sinner can come to Jesus. Thayer reads, "to draw by inward power, lead, impel,"[20] citing John 6:44. Therefore,

19. Coffman, "Commentary on John 6."
20. Thayer, *Greek-English Lexicon*, 204.

Part III: Redemption Applied

it is safe to conclude, "It is not within fallen man's natural ability to come to Christ on his own, without some kind of divine assistance."[21] Moreover, "It is not the freedom of man that comes to the rescue, but the freedom of God. All men would be left in the hopeless position of 'unable to come' *unless* God acts, and He does by drawing men unto Christ."[22] Contra Coffman, it is the sovereign divine action and will that are front and center, not human will or action. Contra Coffman, it is the sovereign action of God's drawing and God's granting that results in people coming. It is the freedom of the Father to draw whosoever he will to the Son, even those whom he has given to the Son from eternity (cf. John 17:24), that Jesus speaks to, not the freedom of humans.

This reading is further substantiated by the parallel passage later in the same chapter. In John 6:65, Jesus reaffirms human inability to come to him unless "it is granted him by the Father." Thus, the ability to come to Jesus is given by the Father to all those he has given to the Son. Once again, contra Dorris, there is no hint of human will except to affirm our inability to come to Jesus in and of ourselves. Indeed, Dorris does not include an additional comment to Lipscomb's comments at this place. So White is correct in concluding, "Outside of this divine enablement . . . no man can come to Christ. No man can 'will' to come to Christ outside this divine drawing."[23] Carson similarly writes, "However much men and women are commanded to believe, and are held accountable for their unbelief, genuine coming to faith is never finally a matter of autonomous human decision."[24] Genuine coming to faith or coming to Christ is finally a matter of autonomous *divine* decision.

Verse 44 also answers why it is Jesus can so definitively affirm, "All that the Father gives Me will come to Me" (v. 37). There is an unbroken chain and harmonious agreement in the work of the Father, the Son, and the Holy Spirit. The Father draws each one ("him") he has given to the Son and perfectly grants each one to come to the Son by the Spirit. Or, to explore the range of meaning for the word "draws," the Father *impels* those he has given to the Son to come to the Son, that is, to believe in him. This impulse

---

21. Sproul, *Chosen by God*, 68. Sproul also supplied the language of "universal negative" and "necessary condition" found in this section (67–68).
22. White, *Potter's Freedom*, 160.
23. White, *Potter's Freedom*, 160.
24. Carson, *John*, 302–3.

to come to the Son is accomplished through the work of the Holy Spirit in convicting, awakening, and regenerating the sinner.

God's action comes first. This is always the case. Specifically, it is the Father's work which is in view and which is the priority. Then, in response to the Father's action, people look to the Son, come to the Son, believe on the Son, and receive eternal life with the confident assurance that they will be raised up on the last day.

> It is written in the Prophets, 'And they will all be taught by God.' Everyone who has heard and learned from the Father comes to me—(John 6:45)

This verse provides us with Jesus' infallible interpretation of Isa 54:13. The text says, "All your sons will be taught of Yahweh" (Isa 54:13, LSB). The LXX is similar, "And all your sons will be instructed by God" (LES 2nd Ed.). The "sons" are the offspring of the "afflicted one" (v. 11). The affliction in view is childlessness since she is called "O barren one" (v. 1). Jerusalem is here personified as a barren women whose Husband, Yahweh, had "for a brief moment" deserted her (v. 7) and "in overflowing anger" he hid his face from her (v. 8a). However, Yahweh says, "With everlasting love I will have compassion on you" (v. 8b). A restoration of fortunes is coming for Yahweh's people. Clearly, this is a prophecy for the post-exilic period. Contextually, it is also linked to the atoning work of the suffering servant (Isa 53). Yahweh would have mercy upon his people and usher in a new Jerusalem full of "sons" who will be taught by Yahweh and will have great peace (v. 13). The "many" whose sins are carried by the servant of Yahweh (53:12) and who are "accounted righteous" due to the work of the servant of Yahweh (53:11) will all be taught by Yahweh God.

This is the text Jesus cites in the hearing of his fellow kinsmen according to the flesh in the synagogue in Capernaum. However, he conspicuously leaves out "your sons," a phrase present in both the Hebrew text and LXX, "presumably in order to accommodate the notion that not only Israelites but also gentiles will be included in the orbit of God's salvation provided by Jesus."[25] This seems reasonable since the context in Isa 54 indicates the international scope of the territory of the children of the barren women. "Your offspring will possess the nations," says the prophet, since they serve "the God of the whole earth" (vs. 3, 5).

---

25. Köstenberger, "John," 450.

Part III: Redemption Applied

As argued above, "all" the ones who are taught by God are "all" those given by the Father to the Son who are drawn by the Father to come to and believe in the Son. Indeed, "all" (*pantes*) corresponds to "everyone" (*pas*) in Jesus' interpretation of the OT Scripture. It is all the ones who have heard and have learned from the Father who have been taught by the Father and consequently come to the Son. Contra Clarke, Pink points out, "The 'all' *does not mean* all of humanity, but all of God's children, all His elect."[26] Not one given by the Father to the Son will fail to hear, learn, and be taught by God; nor will any given by the Father to the Son fail to come to the Son. All those given by the Father to the Son will be drawn by the Father, taught by him, and will come to the Son.

The emphasis in verse 45 is upon God the Father. God is the Agent of instruction since "they will all be taught by God." "By God" translates a genitive of agency, further evidenced by "from the Father" later in the verse. In addition, God is the Agent who enables one to hear and learn. "From the Father" translates *para tou patros*, *para* being a preposition of "agentive source of an activity."[27] This emphasis on God as the agent of teaching is in agreement with verse 44's emphasis on God as the one drawing people to the Son. Furthermore, the objects of divine activity are all the same in verses 44–45. The ones drawn by the Father to the Son whom the Son will raise up on the last day are the same ones taught by the Father and are enabled by the Father hear and learn so as to come to the Son. Any attempt to introduce division among these actions or insert distinctions between the objects of divine activity must reckon with the text itself.

> not that anyone has seen the Father except he who is from God; he has seen the Father. (John 6:46)

Here is the guardrail put in place by our Lord to prevent the abuse of some who appeal to a mystical experience while at the same time answering those who object to what has been put forward concerning the activity of the triune God in bringing about regeneration and faith. How is it that we hear and learn from God? How is it we are taught by God? Especially since no one has seen the Father?

This is a point that John has been consistent on in his gospel. "No one has ever seen God" (1:18). "[The Father's] voice you have never heard, His form you have never seen" (5:37). Therefore, it is not through some

---

26. Pink, *John*, 339.
27. Louw and Nida, *Greek-English Lexicon*, 798.

The Spirit Gives Life to Those Given by the Father to the Son

mystical experience or still, small voice. It is not the burning in the bosom. It is not through a beatific vision. It is not by way of some direct communication with a sinner that the Father teaches or that an individual hears and learns and so comes to Christ.

No one has seen the Father "except He who is from God," that is, the Son, Jesus. Jesus has made the Father known (1:18c). Indeed, he is fully qualified to do this since he is "the only God, who is at the Father's side" (1:18b). He is fully qualified since "He has seen the Father" (6:46). Therefore, the Son has perfect knowledge of the Father and enjoys personal communion with him. In fact, he is very God of very God, even God in himself. Thus, to know the Father we must know the Son.

But how do we know the Son? The Father is known only through his Word. Certainly "the Word became flesh and dwelt among us" (1:14). Thus, knowledge of God is not possible apart from the revelation given in the incarnate Son (cf. Heb 1:2). But how do we know anything about the Word incarnate? Only through the written word. It is through the written word that we come to know the incarnate Word and so come to hear, learn, and be taught by the Father. There is no need for a false dichotomy between the written word and the incarnate Word as some postulate. The written word bears witness to the incarnate Word.

> "Truly, truly, I say to you, whoever believes has eternal life." (John 6:47 ESV)

This verse comes at the end of the argument. Unfortunately, what often happens is this text is read backward into the preceding argument. Also, it is used to assume that humanity has the innate ability to believe. This is why context and a verse-by-verse approach which follows the argument is so vital. Jesus has explained why those who heard him that day in the synagogue in Capernaum did not believe him. He has provided a perspective from above, the divine perspective on unbelief and faith. Hence, only those given to him by the Father come to him (v. 37); he will lose none of those given to him (v. 39); looking to the Son and believing in him is the result of having been given by the Father to the Son (v. 40); indeed, no one is able to come to, i.e., believe in, the Son unless the Father draws that person (v. 44); but all those given by the Father to the Son, whom the Father draws to himself, will be taught by God so as to hear and learn from the Father so that they come to, i.e., believe in, the Son (v. 45). Therefore, the one believing, with all the divine significance such faith has inherent in it, has eternal life.

Part III: Redemption Applied

THE SPIRIT GIVES LIFE TO ALL THOSE GIVEN BY THE FATHER TO THE SON

Up to this point the Spirit has been a silent partner in the work of triune God. The Father and the Son have been the main actors in the work of redemption. The Spirit has not been mentioned. However, the Spirit of God now takes center stage as Jesus teaches that the Spirit gives life to the elect of God. Only by the Spirit can we truly hear the voice of the Father and see him in the Son. This point is only strengthened when the Spirit's work as a whole is considered.

It is later in John that Jesus links the ministry of the Holy Spirit with teaching. Jesus promises his disciples, "But the Helper, the Holy Spirit, whom the Father will send in my name, he will teach you all things and bring to your remembrance all that I have said to you" (John 14:26). The connection to John 6:45, "They will all be taught by God," is strong. Indeed, the future tense, "will teach," corresponds to "they will be" in 6:45. The verbal form of "teach" is used in 14:26 while the noun form was used in 6:45. Thus, it is reasonable to conclude that by the Holy Spirit, who is sent by the Father in the name of the Son, the triune God teaches all those who come to the Son.

Further into the discourse of Jesus on that final night before the cross Jesus promises, "When the Spirit of truth comes, he will guide you into all the truth, for he will not speak on his own authority, but whatever he hears he will speak, and he will declare to you the things that are to come" (John 16:13). This verse has already been explored in its context relative to the harmonious union which exists between the Father, Son, and Holy Spirit. Now the connection to the teaching ministry of the Holy Spirit is accentuated. He will only teach what he has heard (like the Son, cf. 8:28b). He does this by *guiding*, a term which denotes care, like a shepherd leading his flock (cf. Rev 7:17).[28] It may be akin to taking someone by the hand and leading them from one place to the other, perhaps out of darkness and into light. This is a far cry from the caricature which is often portrayed of God "forcing Himself" upon sinners. So the Father by the Spirit "guides" people out of error and falsehood into the truth, even guiding them to the Son.

The OT roots of God guiding his people in connection with his teaching his people are noteworthy. It seems reasonable that our Lord had these

---

28. In LXX, Ps 22:3 (Eng. 23:3) Yahweh the Shepherd "guides me in paths of righteousness."

The Spirit Gives Life to Those Given by the Father to the Son

in mind when he spoke to his disciples. It is likewise safe to conclude that the same Holy Spirit who moved the psalmist to pen these psalms similarly moved John to record the upper room scene. In other words, these links are intentional.

In Ps 25:9 (LXX, 24:9) and also 143:10 (LXX, 142:10), one finds parallels between guiding and teaching. "He leads the humble in what is right, and teaches the humble his way" (Ps 25:9). In LXX, the word for "lead" is the same word John uses in John 16:13 (*hodēgēsei*). Yahweh "leads" or guides, and the parallel construction connects Yahweh's guidance with his teaching. It is also noted that it is "the humble" that Yahweh guides and teaches. "Teach me to do your will, for you are my God! Let your good Spirit lead me on level ground!" (Ps 143:10) As with 25:9, the word for "leads" is the same word used in John 16:13. Especially noteworthy from this verse is that it is the "good Spirit" of God which "guides me on level ground." In fact, in LXX, it is the "holy Spirit" who guides one "in the straight way." So we see that Yahweh by his Spirit "guides" his people. Once again, the guidance of the Holy Spirit is paralleled with teaching in this verse. So it is by the Spirit that people are taught and led by God.

While it is true that exegetically the Spirit has not been mentioned thus far in John 6, when all of Scripture is brought to bear on the work of the triune God in converting sinners, the Holy Spirit is present and active in that work. These foregoing passages help bring this to light. They also help focus the life-giving of the Spirit in the final verses in John 6.

> It is the Spirit who gives life; the flesh is no help at all. The words that I have spoken to you are spirit and life. (John 6:63)

The contrast between the Spirit and the flesh is evident. "It is the Spirit who gives life" affirms in no uncertain terms that it is only God the Holy Spirit who can cause life or make alive. Literally the phrase could be rendered, "The Spirit is the One making alive." Here we have yet another strong affirmation for the deity of the Spirit since it is God "who gives life to all things" (1 Tim 6:13). No life, whether physical or spiritual, exists outside of the sovereign power of the life-giving Holy Spirit. In this context, since so many spiritual actions are in view (faith, coming to Christ, being drawn by the Father) and eternal life has been mentioned numerous times (v. 40, 47, 51 ["live forever"], 54, 58 ["live forever"], 68), the "life" which the Spirit gives is spiritual life.

Part III: Redemption Applied

The truth of spiritual life only through the Spirit is further drilled home in the next phrase: "The flesh is no help at all." This is a grim reminder that left to themselves the disciples can never have life. There is "no help," no assistance, no benefit from the flesh. "Jesus' point here seems to be that human reason unaided by the Spirit is unable to discern what is spiritual."[29] Scripture bears witness that one may have eyes to see that do not see. Or ears to hear that do not hear. Those in the flesh cannot experience life and have no life in them.

Also evident in this text is the close connection between the Spirit of God and the word of God. "The words that I have spoken to you are spirit and life." First, Christ's words are *spirit* in the sense that they are the product of the Spirit. During his lifetime, Christ was dependent upon the resources of the Holy Spirit. Second, since the Spirit is the source of the words, Christ's words are *life*. Spiritual life is produced by the words of Christ because they come from the life-giving Spirit, and the Spirit himself activates these words in those whom the Father has given to the Son.

> But there are some of you who do not believe." (For Jesus knew from the beginning who those were who did not believe, and who it was who would betray him.) (John 6:64)

This verse brings us full circle from where the chapter began: Jesus is explaining the unbelief of the crowds (v. 36). They had witnessed a miracle so spectacular that all four gospel writers record it. They had heard the greatest preacher ever speak words of "spirit and life," even "eternal life" (v. 68). These blessings profited them nothing because they remained in the flesh. Their hearts remained hard, so that although they followed him, they were "grumbling" about his hard saying (v. 60–61). Pink notes, "No man with an *un*changed heart and mind will ever embrace God's salvation."[30] These unbelievers had unchanged hearts.

Implicit in this verse is that while "some of you do not believe," there are others who do believe or at least who would believe. Why would some believe and some disbelieve? The next verse answers this question.

> And he said, "This is why I told you that no one can come to me unless it is granted him by the Father." (John 6:65)

---

29. Köstenberger, "John," 451.
30. Pink, *John*, 337.

The Spirit Gives Life to Those Given by the Father to the Son

"And He said" in the imperfect tense indicates he kept saying to them. This was not a one-time speech; Jesus continued to tell them *why* they persisted in unbelief. Indeed, his words stand written, and he has told us the nature of faith, coming to him, the work of the triune God in bringing the elect to eternal life.

What Jesus kept saying to the crowds concerns the work of the Father in enabling people to come to the Son. The statement is remarkably similar to what Jesus said earlier. There is the universal negative ("no one"); human ability, or lack thereof, is referenced ("can"); there is a necessary condition ("unless"); the action is done by God the Father. The only difference is the verb used.[31] The Father is the one who is doing the action of the verb "granted."[32] The Father is granting people the ability to come to Christ. In other words, all those who come to Christ ultimately come to Christ because the Father has granted them that ability. This is why some believe (i.e., come to Christ): the Father has granted them to believe (cf. Phil 1:29).

Coming to Christ results in life. Since it is the Spirit who gives life (v. 63), it is through the agency of the Spirit that the Father grants people the ability to come to Christ. The Father through the Spirit grants and enables those whom he has given to the Son to come to the Son in due time. The entire Trinity is at work to bring about regeneration.

---

31. In verse 44 the verb is *helkusē* while in verse 65 it is an anarthrous participle *dedomenon* preceded by a verb of being *ē* yielding a paraphrastic construction.

32. Technically, as noted in note 31, this is a paraphrastic construction with a verb of being followed by an anarthrous participle (*ē dedomenon*), the present tense verb and the perfect tense participle yielding a reading with the tense equivalent of a perfect tense.

CHAPTER 10

The Indwelling, Sanctifying Spirit

THE PREVIOUS CHAPTER SHOWED the work of the Spirit in granting new spiritual life (i.e., regeneration). This is situated within a Trinitarian framework: Jesus the Son explained that all those given to him by the Father would come to him as enabled by the life-giving Spirit. The life which is begun by the Spirit is likewise sustained by the Spirit. The Holy Spirit is at work in the heart and life of the believer to perfectly apply the work accomplished by the Son. The Father sends the Spirit of the Son to indwell believers and enable them to pursue holiness. God sends God into our hearts for the work of sanctification.

The Holy Spirit indwelling believers means that God the Holy Spirit takes up residence and is present in the church corporately and Christians individually. Jesus told his disciples that the Holy Spirit ("the Spirit of truth") "dwells with you and will be in you" (John 14:17). At the same time, Jesus likewise promised to those who love him and keep his word that both the Father and the Son "will come to him and make our home with him" (John 14:23). The presence of all three persons of the one God is promised to believers. Yet it is by the agency of the Holy Spirit that the triune God indwells believers (see Acts 2:38; 1 Cor 3:16–17; 6:19, et al). God's indwelling is Trinitarian by means of the Holy Spirit.

The indwelling Spirit is present in believers to help them (John 14:16) and for the very important work of sanctifying God's people. Sanctification means to make holy, set apart, separate so as to designate for a particular

The Indwelling, Sanctifying Spirit

purpose. When applied to the indwelling Spirit, sanctification is the Spirit's work of conforming believers to the image of Christ. There are three dimensions to the Christian's sanctification, all of which the Spirit is involved in. First, there is positional (or definite) sanctification. From the moment of conversion when we are united to Christ, our status changes from unholy to holy (1 Cor 6:11). Second, there is progressive (or ongoing) sanctification. This is what most of people think of when it comes to sanctification and it will be the primary focus of this chapter. Progressive sanctification is the Holy Spirit's ongoing supernatural work to rid believers of the disease of sin, conform us to Christ's image, and empower us for good works. Finally, there is perfect (or final) sanctification. This is when we are in glory, completely purged of sin and fully conformed to the image of Christ (1 Thess 5:23). In all three dimensions of sanctification, the indwelling Spirit is at work to sanctify his people.[1]

As has been demonstrated thus far, the work of God is the work of the triune God. Therefore, the whole Trinity works together harmoniously to accomplish their ends. This means that when it comes to the work of the Spirit in sanctification, the Holy Spirit is working out the eternal purpose of the triune God in time in believers. Sanctification is God's work: "Now may the God of peace Himself sanctify you completely" (1 Thess 5:23). The person within the Trinity who takes the primary role in the work of sanctification, the agent whereby God carries through his sanctifying work, is the Holy Spirit.

THE FATHER SENDS THE SPIRIT OF THE SON INTO OUR HEARTS

It is recognized by most that chapters 3–4 of Galatians are Paul's defense of the doctrine of justification by faith along doctrinal grounds. It begins with a personal appeal to the Galatians (3:1–5) with several pointed questions including, "Did you receive the Spirit by works of the law or by hearing with faith?" (v. 2). Paul then moves to the Scriptures (3:6–14), quoting from Gen 15:6; 12:3; Deut 27:26; Hab 2:4; Lev 18:5; and Deut 21:23. He then reasons from the Scriptures and the Law itself (3:15–22) that the promise is given to those who have faith (v. 22). At this point (3:23–24:7) the argument shifts

---

1. These three dimensions of sanctification can be found, for example, in Peterson, *Salvation Applied*, 336.

Part III: Redemption Applied

to the practical application of the promise to his readers and himself.[2] One significant change which has taken place with Paul and his readers is that they have gone from slaves to sons (4:1–7): "we also . . . were enslaved" (v. 3), but now "you are sons" (v. 6).

Two key events, heavy with Trinitarian overtones, caused this change. First, "God sent forth His Son" (4:4). That is, God the Father sent forth God the Son. God sent God into the world to accomplish redemption (4:5). This is the coming of Christ into the world. Second, "God sent the Spirit of His Son" (4:6). That is, God the Father sent God the Holy Spirit. God sent God into the world to apply redemption to those who have received adoption. This is the coming of the Holy Spirit into the world, especially into the hearts of believers.

> And because you are sons, God has sent the Spirit of his Son into our hearts, crying, "Abba! Father!" (Gal 4:6)

The Father sent the Son into the world in the fullness of time (4:4). Then, the Father (with the Son, Acts 2:33) sends the Spirit of his Son into the hearts of those who have received adoption as sons (4:5b). Indeed, it is by the Holy Spirit that the Father and the Son likewise dwell in the believer (cf. John 14:23). Where the Spirit is, there is the Father and the Son also.

Here the Holy Spirit is called "the Spirit of His Son." All at once in this phrase the Trinity is in view. The Son is the Father's Son ("His Son"). The Spirit is the Son's Spirit ("the Spirit of the Son"). The Son's Spirit is sent by the Father ("God has sent"). Careful distinction is made between the persons of the Trinity while maintaining unity of purpose in God. Further, the sending of the Son (v. 4) and the Spirit (v. 6) does not communicate inequality where the Father is superior to the Son and the Spirit (with the Son and Spirit being inferior). Rather, by mutual consent from before time began, the Son willingly determined to be sent by the Father to redeem the Father's children, and the Spirit likewise willingly determined to be sent by the Father to sanctify those same children.

It is the Holy Spirit the Father sends into the hearts of the redeemed. The Son is sent by the Father "to redeem" (v. 5) and the Spirit is sent by the Father into the hearts of the redeemed. It is in the heart that the Spirit does his regenerating work. Foolish hearts he makes wise unto salvation.

---

2. From 3:6–22 the argument has been more abstract in third person (e.g., "those who are of faith" [v. 9] and "those who believe" [v. 22]). At 3:23 the pronouns enter the fray ("we," "our," "you") as Paul addresses his readers and himself as the very ones he had been talking about up to that point, viz., those who believe.

The Indwelling, Sanctifying Spirit

Darkened hearts he illuminates with the light of the gospel. Hard hearts of stone he takes out and replaces with a heart of flesh.

Such heart-work is essential because the heart is the seat of our nature whereby affections/desires are produced. Everything about us is tied to the heart. Every aspect of our nature has been touched by sin. Specifically, human hearts are hardened (Eph 4:18), darkened (Rom 1:21), callous (Eph 4:19), foolish (Rom 1:21), evil, and unbelieving (Heb 3:12). Far from having a "good heart," humans have a heart problem. Absent the Spirit's work we love and want the wrong things. The Holy Spirit is sent into our hearts by the Father in order to change our hearts, remove the heart of stone and put in a heart of flesh, even giving us a new heart (Ezek 36:26). We cannot give ourselves a new heart or perform the required spiritual heart surgery; only God the Holy Spirit can and does do this for believers.

The result of the new heart is new desires and affections produced by the Holy Spirit within us. One new desire produced by the Spirit relates to prayer. The Spirit in our hearts cries, "Abba, Father." Previous to our conversion we would not want God as Father. Indeed, as seen, we loved darkness and were by nature children of the Father's wrath. But with the coming of the Spirit into our hearts, we call on God as "Abba, Father." Whereas we once hated God, now we love him as Father. Whereas we once were faithless, we now put our faith in God as Father. Whereas we once rebelled, now we obey God as Father. In short, we want the Father. This is a new desire produced within us by the Holy Spirit.

There is nothing potential here with the sending of the Holy Spirit. The Father "has sent" the Holy Spirit into our hearts. It is the exact same word in the exact same form as "sent forth" in verse 4 in reference to the Son. In the same way that the Son was sent forth into the world to accomplish his mission, so too the Holy Spirit is sent forth into the hearts of believer's to fulfill his sanctifying purpose. Said another way: "The salvation that was *bought* for God's people by the Son will not avail except it be also *wrought* in their *hearts* by that Son's Spirit."[3] Any interpretation which would seek to rob the believer of the real presence of the Holy Spirit in her heart must likewise be applied to the Son and his work in coming to earth.[4] But such interpretations jeopardize our salvation at minimum.

---

3. Hendriksen and Kistemaker, *Exposition of Galatians*, 161. Emphasis original.

4. This is an important point because within the Restoration Movement there is a branch of churches who deny the indwelling of the Holy Spirit. References to the Holy Spirit dwelling in Christians in the New Testament are reduced to mere historical footnotes of significance only for the first century church, related to miraculous spiritual gifts

Part III: Redemption Applied

Moreover, the truth contained here is of tremendous assurance to the believer. The verb tense (aorist) views God's sending of the Holy Spirit into the believer's heart as a single complete work. God has sent his Spirit into the heart of the believer with no intention of taking him back. The Spirit continues to cry out "Abba, Father" with no intention of stopping. We unite in our spirits with this testimony (Rom 8:15). This is proof positive of our adoption. The Father will not deny his children.

It is the Holy Spirit who cries out or shouts in our hearts, "Abba, Father!" We would not and could not call God "Abba, Father" prior to our conversion. The Father through the Son redeemed us "so that we might receive adoption as sons" (4:5). Our ability to call God "Abba, Father" as well as our desire to call him such is due to the change in our relationship to God effected by the completed work of the Son and the ongoing work of the Holy Spirit in our hearts.

THE SPIRIT SANCTIFIES BELIEVERS

Sanctification is God's work (1 Thess 5:23). Just as the Son took the lead in the work of redemption by taking on human nature so that he might die in our place for our sins, so the Holy Spirit takes the lead in the work of sanctification by coming into our hearts so that we are changed to be sons of God.

> But we ought always to give thanks to God for you, brothers beloved by the Lord, because God chose you as the firstfruits to be saved, through sanctification by the Spirit and belief in the truth. To this he called you through our gospel, so that you may obtain the glory of our Lord Jesus Christ. (2 Thess 2:13–14)

This is the second prayer of thanksgiving by Paul for the Thessalonian Christians (see 1:3). Paul here thanks God for these Christians in Thessalonica "because God chose you from the beginning for salvation" (NASB). It must not be overlooked that God is the one who does the action ("chose"). The object of God's choice is "you," i.e., the believers who comprise "the church in Thessalonica" (1:1).

These Christians are "brothers beloved by the Lord." "Lord" in Paul's writing is usually the Lord Jesus Christ (so throughout 2 Thessalonians, see esp. 2:1, 16). So Paul affirms that these Christians are "beloved" by the Son. The force of the verb is that they have been loved and continue to be loved

---

or inspiration of the Holy Spirit. See Camp, *Holy Spirit in Redemption*; Taylor, *Holy Spirit*.

The Indwelling, Sanctifying Spirit

by the Lord (perfect tense). It is this divine love which informs divine election. The choice of God is rooted in the love of the Lord. These Christians are loved by the Son and chosen by the Father "for salvation."

All of this reminiscent of 1 Thess 1:3–5, another thanksgiving prayer of Paul to "our God and Father" wherein he affirms these siblings are loved by God and chosen by God (v. 4). In 2 Thess 2:13, there is no discussion as to why God loved and chose those who are saved. The closest one may get to an explanation is in the use of the middle voice in the verb.[5] The choice by God for salvation from the beginning is for himself. Indeed, the sanctified heart of the saved prays, "Help us, O God of our salvation, for the glory of Your Name, deliver us, and atone for our sins, for Your Name's sake" (Ps 79:9). The sanctified heart of the saved person knows that God saves his people "for His Name's sake, that He might make known His mighty power" (Ps 106:8). For the sanctified heart of the saved person, this is reason enough to answer the why question, not just the question, "Why would God save this person or that person?" but especially the question, "Why would God save *any* sinners?"

Such an answer, though, is insufficient for some. For example, Burton Coffman commenting on this text writes, "God chose all men to be saved, in the sense that every man ever born on earth was destined to be a child of God; but the freedom of the human will nullifies that eternal decree in many. In the New Testament, as here, God's choosing implies also the believer's having accepted."[6] Several things must be said in response to this.

First, the text does *not* say that God chose *all men*; it says, "God chose you." The "you" is specific and confined to the church in Thessalonica (2 Thess 1:1). This is an epistle addressed to Christians. Therefore, it is not "all men" who are in view in God's election but these "brothers beloved by the Lord." Coffman is reading "all men" into "you," which is an eisegetical fallacy.

Second, Coffman assumes not only the freedom of the will in humans, but endues it with the almighty power to thwart, even nullify, the divine will. "Many," says Coffman, nullify God's eternal decree. Such impotence on God's part is absolutely shocking. Equally shocking is the volitional power of humans to annul the divine decree. Further, this conclusion on Coffman's part is out of sync with a plethora of other Scriptures (e.g., Job 5:12; Ps 2:3–4; 33:10–11; Prov 16:9; 19:21; 21:30; Isa 14:24; Dan 4:34–35).

---

5. "Chose" translates *heilato*, an aorist middle indicative verb.
6. Coffman, "2 Thessalonians 2."

Part III: Redemption Applied

Perhaps no verse so soundly refutes Coffman's statement than Isa 14:27: "For Yahweh of hosts has purposed, and who will annul it?"

Third, the only thing implied by God's election is the freedom of God to chose whomever he wills. But even if God's choice of certain people (i.e., those beloved by the Lord) implied anything about those people, it implies their absolute unworthiness to merit such a choice on God's part. Sinners do not deserve election. Acceptance of God's choice is completely absent from this text. Nevertheless, even if one were to entertain acceptance of anything from God on the part of believers, it must be within the framework of the powerful working of the Spirit in them first to enable them to accept it from God. This is seen in the rest of the verse.

There is a textual variant in 2:13. "Firstfruits" is translated "from the beginning" by most other versions (NASB, NIV, KJV). The difference lies in different readings in the manuscripts.[7] Close attention to this variant is outside the scope of this book.

The structure of the next phrases should be carefully noted. Salvation is first "through sanctification by the Spirit." The Spirit's sanctifying work comes first. Then, "belief in the truth." Without a doubt the Thessalonians believed in the truth of the gospel. Their faith was theirs. When it comes to the work of God "for salvation" (LSB), the Spirit's action of sanctification sets the whole process in motion. Only then are people enabled to believe the truth. Before the Thessalonians believed in the truth, the Spirit of God was powerfully at work to cause regeneration unto salvation. Regeneration precedes faith.

"Belief in the truth" stands in contrast with those who are perishing and "refused to love the truth and so be saved" (v. 10). They loved their sin ("had pleasure in unrighteousness" and "did not believe the truth" [v. 12]). However, those Thessalonians whom the Father chose, upon whom the Lord had set his affection, and whom the Spirit set apart were those who, when they heard the truth, believed it.

"He called you" means God called these Christians. The means of God for saving those he loved, chose, and called is the gospel ("through the gospel"). As Gene Green writes, "The God who chose them to be saved is the same God who made sure that the message of salvation reached them by

---

7. The difference is between whether the reading is *aparchēn* ("firstfruits") or *ap archēs* ("from the beginning"). The manuscripts are split in the evidence, making a decision difficult, though the latter seems slightly preferred by the English translations despite the reading in the critical text.

The Indwelling, Sanctifying Spirit

means of the apostolic proclamation of the gospel."[8] Through and through, from start to finish, the gospel is the glorious work of God.

The phrase "so that you may obtain the glory of our Lord Jesus Christ" points us forward to the glorification of the redeemed. This will be covered more fully in later chapters. Briefly it can be noted that the work of the triune God terminates in the glorification of a particular people. The redeemed of God will experience a state of glory comparable to that of the Lord Jesus Christ himself. The Father who chose, the Son who loved, and the Spirit who sanctifies will not fail to see to it that their people obtain Christ's glory.

We note in closing once again that the Trinity is united in their work of redemption. Those loved by the Son are chosen by the Father. These same ones are sanctified by the Spirit in due time. As they hear the call of the gospel, the Spirit works in those loved by the Son and chosen by the Father to bring about salvation and faith in them. What is accomplished in time for believers points forward also to the glorious revelation of the Lord Jesus Christ. This glory is the end of the Spirit's sanctifying work in the redeemed of God.

---

8. Green, *Thessalonians*, 327.

PART IV

Redemption Glorified

THE GOSPEL ENDS WITH God. Specifically, it ends with the triune God glorifying himself in eternity future. The work of the Trinity in salvation ends in eternity.

God glorifies God in the glorification of his people. The Father is glorified when his children, whom the Son died for and the Spirit sanctified, are brought to their final home. The Son is glorified when he glorifies his brethren, filled with the Spirit, before his Father. The Spirit is glorified when those whom he set apart in the Son are finally presented to the Father.

The ultimate end of the work of redemption is the glory of God.[1] The triune God does what he does throughout history "to the praise of His glorious grace . . . to the praise of His glory" (Eph 1:6, 12, 14). The triune God is up to one thing in the redemption of people across all of time and history: the mutual glorification of the Father, the Son, and the Holy Spirit.

Heaven is a world of love. Heaven is the residence of the triune God who exists from eternity in a mutual loving relationship. The Father loves the Son and the Spirit; the Son loves the Father and the Spirit; the Spirit loves the Father and the Son. It was from this overflow of love that they created the universe and brought about new creation. It will be this overflow of love that the glorified saints will experience and enjoy. Having been purged of all that causes us to love imperfectly, we will join in divine love and perfectly express our love for the Trinity.

---

1. See Edwards, *End for Which God Created the World*, 203–7, for an unpacking of God's glory as the last end of his providential work.

Chapter 11

The Glorification of the Redeemed

Romans 8 is a key text focused on the glorification of those redeemed in Christ. Verses 28–30 will be given special attention in the next chapter. For now, it will suffice to note that earlier in this climatic chapter the work of the Trinity is glorifying particular people.

Romans 8 is the climax of Paul's progressive doctrinal masterpiece. It expands upon the deliverance he mentioned at the close of chapter 7 (v. 24). Those who are in Christ Jesus are not under condemnation (8:1). These operate under a different principle: the Spirit. For several verses (vs. 3–9), Paul juxtaposes the flesh (the anti-God principle in every human being) and the Spirit. As a result of the Spirit's presence in the believer they are able to submit to God's law and do what is pleasing to God (vs. 7–8). Indeed, those in the Spirit belong to Christ (v. 9). We have new life in the Spirit (v. 10). At this point, we are reminded of the already-not yet aspect of the Christian life. While we *already* have life in the Spirit, we have *not yet* experienced the resurrection of the body (hence, "the body is dead because of sin," v. 10a). This leads to verse 11 which addresses the resurrection of the dead:

> If the Spirit of him who raised Jesus from the dead dwells in you, he who raised Christ Jesus from the dead will also give life to your mortal bodies through his Spirit who dwells in you. (Rom 8:11)

Notice the Trinitarian emphasis in this verse: the Holy Spirit dwells in us, he who raised Jesus from the dead is the Father, and the resurrected

Jesus is God the Son. The same power which the Father used to resurrect the Son is the same power at work by the Father to give life to our bodies through the Spirit who lives in the believer.

The Holy Spirit who dwells in us is the resurrecting Spirit: he "raised Jesus from the dead." The fact of the Spirit's involvement in the resurrection of Jesus is stressed twice. Mention of the resurrection of Jesus informs the phrase "will also give life to your mortal bodies." Moo writes, "Since reference to resurrection is so plain in the first part of the sentence, 'will make alive' must also refer to future bodily transformation—through resurrection for dead believers—rather than, for instance, spiritual vivification in justification, or to the 'mortification' of sin in the Christian life."[1] What is in view is our own resurrection. Our bodies are "mortal," that is, subject to death. But with the Spirit within the believer, they have the hope of resurrection from the dead. Christ's resurrection by the Spirit points us to our own resurrection from the dead by the same Spirit. The Spirit gives life to the "mortal bodies" of Christians. The prerequisite for resurrection unto life is the presence of the Holy Spirit within the believer.

In light of the resurrection of the body, there are certain obligations placed upon the believer in this life now (vs. 12–16). We live the Spirit-filled life by putting to death the deeds of the body (v. 13). Christians are led by the Spirit as sons of God (v. 14). The believer's reception of the Holy Spirit is stressed by Paul (v. 15). Then, Paul points to the present work of the Spirit in the children of God which anticipates future glory:

> The Spirit himself bears witness with our spirit that we are children of God, and if children, then heirs—heirs of God and fellow heirs with Christ, provided we suffer with him in order that we may also be glorified with him. (Rom 8:16–17 ESV)

Once more we see the Trinitarian emphasis: the Holy Spirit in the believer with our spirit confirms our identity as children of God ("Abba, Father!" v. 15b), we are children and heirs of God our Father, and we are joint heirs with Christ the Son. Salvation, sanctification, and glorification are the work of the triune God.

One implication drawn from this text is that not everyone has the Spirit dwelling in them. Only Christians have the Spirit dwelling within them. This means not everyone has this witness from the Spirit within them. This means not everyone is a member of God's family, a key point

---

1. Moo, *Romans*, 493.

The Glorification of the Redeemed

to keep in mind later in the chapter when verse 28 is looked at in the next chapter; the promises contained in that text are only "for those who love God." Specific to this text (v. 16), not all people are children of God. All humans are the creations of the creator, viz. "we are all His offspring" (Acts 17:28). But only Christians, who have the Holy Spirit dwelling in them, have the Spirit testifying that they are children of God.

However, since believers are children, all Christians are heirs of God who await their inheritance. All Christians have an inheritance. Both phrases—"God's heirs and Christ's joint-heirs"—indicate possession. God has believers as heirs, and Christ has believers as co-heirs. Being their possession, all that is theirs belongs to Christians. Therefore, the future inheritance is promised to God's heirs and Christ's joint-heirs.

The end of verse 17 introduces the future glory anticipated by the saints of God. But the path to glory is not easy. The road to glory traverses the way of suffering (cf. Acts 14:22). Christ himself suffered in the flesh (cf. 1 Pet 4:1). His followers will likewise "suffer with Him" in the world. Human persecution and angelic opposition produce the suffering that Christians experience in "this present time" (v. 18). But what a comforting thought that whatever suffering the Christian endures, we endure that suffering with Christ. Moreover, glory awaits suffering saints. Mention of this future glory leads Paul to continue:

> For I consider that the sufferings of this present time are not worth comparing with the glory that is to be revealed to us. (Rom 8:18)

Whatever we suffer in the here and now is "not worth comparing with the glory that is to be revealed to us." The future glory the saints of God will experience and enjoy is incomparable. This "glory" is beyond comparison, indeed, it is beyond description and comprehension. This is because it really is altogether different than anything we know in this life.

Jonathan Edwards wrote much on the glory of heaven. One of his works, *Heaven is a World of Love*, emphasizes the infinite, unending, indescribable Trinitarian love that awaits the Christian:

> There, even in heaven, dwells the God from whom every stream of holy love, yea, every drop that is or ever was, proceeds. There dwell God the Father, God the Son, and God the Spirit, united as one in infinitely dear, incomprehensible, mutual, and eternal love. There dwells God the Father, who is the Father of mercies, and so the Father of love, who so loved the world as to give his only begotten Son to die for it. There dwells Christ, the Lamb of God, the Prince

of Peace and of love, who so loved the world that he shed his blood and poured out his soul unto death for men. There dwells the great Mediator, through whom all the divine love is expressed toward men, by whom the fruits of that love have been purchased, through whom they are communicated, and through whom love is imparted to the hearts of all God's people. There dwells Christ in both his natures, the human and the divine, sitting on the same throne with the Father. And there dwells the Holy Spirit, the Spirit of divine love, in whom the very essence of God, as it were, flows out and is breathed forth in love, and by whose immediate influence all holy love is shed abroad in the hearts of all the saints on earth and in heaven. There, in heaven, this infinite fountain of love—this eternal three in one—is set open without any obstacle to hinder access to it as it flows forever. There this glorious God is manifested and shines forth in full glory, in beams of love. And there this glorious fountain forever flows forth in streams, yea, in rivers of love and delight, and these rivers swell, as it were, to an ocean of love, in which the souls of the ransomed may bathe with the sweetest enjoyment, and their hearts, as it were, be deluged with love![2]

The infinite and eternal love which exists between the Father, the Son, and the Holy Spirit will be the ever-increasing experience of the saints in glory. This is why the "glory to be revealed to us" is beyond comparison.

---

2. Edwards, *Heaven*, 36–38.

CHAPTER 12

The Golden Chain of Redemption

> For those whom he foreknew he also predestined to be conformed to the image of his Son, in order that he might be the firstborn among many brothers. And those whom he predestined he also called, and those whom he called he also justified, and those whom he justified he also glorified. (Rom 8:29–30)

MANY HAVE CALLED THIS text "The Golden Chain of Redemption." And for good reason. It presents God's work in redemption as an unbroken golden chain which links eternity past to eternity future. The final phrase in v. 28 ("called according to purpose") introduced the doctrines of foreknowledge, predestination, calling, and glorification. Verses 29–30 are the unfolding of the God's purpose beginning with foreknowledge and terminating in glorification. When Paul elaborates on these themes in vs. 29–30, he is doing so from the divine perspective. This is the perspective of the one who declares the end from the beginning and "from ancient times things not yet done" (Isa 46:10). In addition, what God predestines according to his purpose cannot be thwarted (Isa 14:27). So Paul's purpose as he writes of the divine perspective, from eternity to eternity, is to assure each and every believer concerning God's purpose, namely, God is working together all things for their good and for their glory. That purpose spans all of history from eternity past when God "foreknew" his own people to eternity future when the saints are "glorified" by God.

Part IV: Redemption Glorified

The chain begins with God. Every action in these verses is a divine action. God does all these actions: he foreknew, he predestined, he called, he justified, and he glorified. Therefore, everything studied so far—the work of the Trinity before time and in time—meets in this text with a view of the consummation of the work of God at the end of time.

First, God *foreknew*. "For" (*hoti*) shows a connection to the preceding verse. The mention of "those who are called according to His purpose" stimulates Paul to elaborate on God's purpose from the divine perspective. "He foreknew" means "God foreknew." Since "His Son" is mentioned later in the verse, the Father is the subject of the verb. Hence, God the Father foreknew "those who are called according to His purpose," i.e., his children (the Son's "many brothers"). Given the linguistic data concerning "foreknew," what is presented here is a tender picture of God's special love for his children from all eternity.[1] "Those whom" (*hous*) shows the personal nature of God's foreknowledge. It is people, not plans or events, who are the object of God's foreknowledge. Moo notes, "Paul does not say that God knew anything *about* us but that he knew *us*."[2] God foreknew people, his people, the ones called according to purpose.

Second, God *predestined*. Some translations say, "foreordained." As with "He foreknew," God is the subject of the verb "He predestined" (*proōrisen*). The same objects of divine action are in view, i.e., "those who" (*hous*). There is no break or division in the text. Hence, God predestined those whom he foreknew. The people God foreknew are the same ones he predestined.

Paul specifies that God has predestined those whom he foreknew to conformity to the image of his Son. Most English translations supply a verb such as "to be" (ESV) or "to become" (LSB) to clarify God's intention in predestination.[3] Dunn is correct that in view is "the anticipated outcome of the resurrection of the body . . . the end result of the process (complete conformity to Christ's death, complete transformation into his likeness . . . It is the sureness of the end as determined from the beginning which Paul wishes to emphasize."[4] God's predestining work is for the believer's ("we,"

---

1. See Schreiner, *Romans*, 452; Dunn, *Romans 1–8*, 482. More on the linguistic data below in the analysis.

2. Moo, *Romans*, 532. Emphasis original.

3. Since the latter part of the verse has *einai*, "to be," it seems reasonable that the verb implied in the early part of the verse would be the same.

4. Dunn, *Romans 1–8*, 483.

"us," vs. 28, 31) future glory. That future glory consists of total conformity to the Son's glorious image.

The end of verse 29 further drives home the divine intention. Intentionality is evident in the adverbial use of the infinitive in the phrase *eis to einai*. The preposition *eis* with the articular infinitive can indicate purpose or result. The phrase is translated "so that He would be" (LSB).[5] The Father's intention of foreknowing and conforming those who believe to the image of his Son is for the purpose of the Son being "firstborn," a word which emphasizes Christ's preeminence. The preeminent status of the Son among his many brothers was the intention of the Father before time began when he foreknew those who would be conformed to the image of the Son. In this way, the Son is the "firstborn among many brothers."

Third, God *called*. As with the foregoing two verbs, "He called" has God as the subject. Moreover, the same objects are in view as with the preceding phrases: "those who" (*hous*), i.e., those foreknown and predestined by God to conformity to Christ's image. Only certain select individuals fit this description. In addition, this calling is couched between the preceding actions of God (viz., foreknew and predestined) and "He justified" (to be considered shortly). These links militate against a common view that a general or universal call of God is in view.

Fourth, God *also justified*. As with "foreknew," "predestined," and "called," God is the subject of the verb "He justified." Nothing in the text indicates a break in the objects of God's actions: the same ones foreknown and predestined and called are likewise justified. Those who are called by God in time are also justified by God in Christ.

Finally, God *also glorified*. As with all the foregoing verbs, God is the subject of the verb "He glorified" (*edoxasen*). Moreover, the same objects are in view, viz., those called according to God's purpose who are foreknown, predestined, called, and justified. So these same ones who God justified in Christ are the same ones whom God glorifies. There is no break or division between these actions of God and nothing in the verse warrants breaking the golden chain of redemption. Travis Campbell summarizes Paul's argument succinctly: "*In this context*, there is no such thing as a person foreknown who is not also predestined, one predestined who is not also called,

---

5. The ESV's "in order that he might be" starts off well, but the "might" hints at a possibility of failure absent from Paul's presentation here.

one called who is not also justified, one justified who is not also glorified. In the divine mind, it is all a done deal."[6]

ANALYSIS OF CHURCH OF CHRIST INTERPRETATION OF ROM 8:29–30

Several attempts, both from within and without the Stone-Campbell Movement, have sought to explain these verses in such a way that the force of what is said is diminished. This section will present various explanations offered which seek to avoid particular conclusions deemed "too Calvinistic," with a special emphasis on Restoration Movement literature.

Problems with God's Purpose

Within the churches of Christ, one commentator on the book of Romans who has governed how we read 8:28–30 is Moses E. Lard. His commentary is referenced numerous times by Coffman, especially for Rom 8:28–30. Lard uses the phrase "called according to purpose" as the lens through which verses 29–30 are read. On this phrase he writes, "*Prothesis* here rendered *purpose* is from *prostithemi*, which means to place out or set before. Accordingly *prothesis* means a placing or setting before."[7]

Several problems are inherent in Lard's presentation. First, Lard says the noun *prothesin* found in Rom 8:28 is from the verb *prostithēmi*. This simply is wrong on several counts. First, *prothesin* is the accusative form of *prothesis*; *prothesis* is not "from" *prostithemi*. Second, even if that were the case, *prostithemi* does not mean "to place out or set before." The lexicons have "to put to, "to add," or "join together," not placing before. What seems to be happening is that Lard is falling prey to the root fallacy and/or the compound word fallacy. He takes *pros*, a preposition which could mean "before," and the verb *tithēmi*, which can mean "to place," and assumes that together they can mean "to place/set before." However, the word *prostithēmi* simply does not mean that as lexical sources easily demonstrate. In short, to illustrate the point, *prostithēmi* no more means "to place before" than profound means "to find before." Third, *prothesis* has a definite meaning. One definition of *prothesis* is, as Lard identifies, "setting forth" or "putting

---

6. Campbell, *Wonderful Decree*, 87. Emphasis original.
7. Lard, *Romans*, 280. Emphasis original.

out" (though notably without reference to "before"). However, words have a range of meaning, and which meaning is in view depends upon the context. Further, lexicons include more than one definition for the term, including "that which is planned in advance, *plan, purpose, resolve, will*."[8] Romans 8:28 is specifically cited with reference to divine purpose. Therefore, immediately, due to substantial linguistic and lexical errors, including a faulty definition of "purpose," Lard is off target from the start.

Lard then uses his erroneous definition of *prothesis* to argue that God's purpose means God having everything—humans, redemption, destinies—set or placed before him mentally. In his mind and in eternity, as Lard acknowledges, God has "complete view of the future."[9] This enables God to "foresee" what Lard calls "ideal not actual persons" as well as "their own choice." So he writes, God "foresaw in the *prothesis* that certain persons would, of their own choice, obey him or his Son; that they would comply with the conditions of justification, and so be saved. These were the persons 'whom he foreknew.' They were therefore ideal not actual persons. They existed in *prothesis*, not in fact; still all that God did of them was as real as though they had been actual persons."[10] First, as demonstrated this view of God's purpose is foreign to Rom 8:28. Second, philosophical categories of humans, categories foreign to the context, are smuggled in resulting in God foreknowing not *actual* people, only *ideal* persons. Humans are dehumanized and depersonalized according to this scheme. Third, all that God did for these non-actual people is somehow real, though how is not explained. Might it be because there is no way to explain how God can perform real actions on non-actual persons? Fourth, Lard reduces God's action of foreknowing to mere prescience ("foresaw"), though he attempts to salvage it with a sentence about the word also meaning "approving and accepting."[11] However, as demonstrated above, when Paul says God "foreknew" it means he "foreloved" his people. One is once again puzzled how God can then truly forelove persons who are neither actual nor factual, but merely ideal, however that is defined.

Going further, like so many within the Restoration Movement, a premium is placed on human free will by Lard. He smuggles the idea into the text of Rom 8:28–30 though it is absent from the text itself. Thus,

8. BDAG, 869.
9. Lard, *Romans*, 281.
10. Lard, *Romans*, 282.
11. Lard, *Romans*, 282.

Part IV: Redemption Glorified

> In that *prothesis*, accordingly, each man was as distinctly before God, as saved or lost, as he will be when the judgment is past; not because God decreed that this man should be saved and that one not, but because, leaving each absolutely free to choose his own destiny, he could and did as certainly foresee what that destiny would be, as though he himself had fixed it by unchangeable decree.[12]

One is left to wonder what exactly it is God *did* decree. Apparently, the only thing unchangeably decreed according to God's (free) will is that humans will be "absolutely free." Later, Lard writes, "In the matter of their obedience, [God] left them *wholly uninfluenced* by any predetermining act of his; that is, *he left them free*. Yet he foresaw that they would do his will; and *it was because of this, their own voluntary act*, that he predetermined them."[13] Here is the key determining factor in God's predestining work: human free will. Lard, like so many within the Restoration Movement, makes it so that the creature (pre)determines the creator's actions. So that there is no confusion, Lard doubles down on affirming the almighty will of the creature: "[God's] act of predetermination was determined by their voluntary act of obedience."[14] The tail wags the dog! The creature controls his creator. If you choose wrong, God is stuck "as though he himself had fixed it by unchangeable decree," to borrow the phrase from Lard. Conversely, since you chose correctly "in that *prothesis*," you determined God's act and, in fact, because of that good choice, merited the predetermining action of God. Congratulations! You just earned your salvation.

Every single aspect of Lard's interpretation of Rom 8:28–30 is faulty. Grammatically it is wrong. Its emphasis on philosophical categories is unwarranted. When it comes to "free will," we must affirm God's will is freest. He is sinless, holy, and perfect. He alone is wise. We, on the other hand, are sinful, unholy, and imperfect. Left to our own devices, we would never choose God. Therefore, when it comes to free will, for humans it is highly overrated. But this is a typical position for Restoration Movement thinkers: an overvaluation of free will. This is often accompanied by a poor or absent definition of what free will is.

---

12. Lard, *Romans*, 281.
13. Lard, *Romans*, 282. Emphasis mine.
14. Lard, *Romans*, 282.

The Golden Chain of Redemption

Defining Foreknowledge

There are common explanations of what is meant by "God foreknew." One explanation says God foreknows events. God's foreknowledge is mere prescience in this case. For example, Coffman, after a quote from Godet, writes, "The only thing meant by the word 'foreknew' in this verse is that God knew in advance all that would happen."[15] Thus, when God *foreknew* what is meant is God *foresees*. It is sometimes presented as follows: From eternity God looks down the corridors of time and sees beforehand those who would believe in Christ.

In response, while it is true that the word "foreknew" *can* mean simple prescience (e.g., Acts 26:5; 2 Pet 3:17), when God is the subject of the word it means more than that (see Rom 11:2; Acts 2:23; 1 Pet 1:2, 20). In addition, the relationship between the Greek root (*proginōskō*) with the Old Testament verb "to know" (Heb. *yada*) is well-attested. Boyd recognizes these linguistic connections when he writes, "In customary Semitic fashion, Paul seems to be using the word *know* to mean 'intimately love.'"[16] While his open theism is suspect, Boyd's linguistic analysis here is solid. God's foreknowledge is more than mere intellectual knowledge; it is relational knowledge. Hence, God fore*loves* his people. Also, Coffman's scope for what God foreknew is too wide when he writes "God knew in advance *all that would happen.*" I do not disagree that Scripture teaches God has exhaustive knowledge of all things (1 John 3:20; Heb 4:13). However, Rom 8:29 does not teach that. The scope of God's foreknowledge here is "those." As Moo observes, "It is only *some* individuals—those who, having been 'foreknown,' were also 'predestined,' 'called,' 'justified,' and 'glorified'—who are the objects of this activity; and this shows that an action applicable only to Christians must be denoted by the verb."[17] Morris likewise affirms, "God's knowledge of [the saved] is not the same as his foreknowledge of all mankind."[18] Therefore, it is Christians whom God knows and loves intimately beforehand which leads to their being predestined.

Before predestination is addressed, though, another common reading of "foreknew" should be addressed. Some argue God foreknows a group, as distinct from individuals. So Coffman also writes, "Paul here did not

---

15. Coffman, "Commentary on Romans 8."
16. Boyd, *God of the Possible*, 48.
17. Moo, *Romans*, 533.
18. Morris, *Romans*, 332.

Part IV: Redemption Glorified

speak of individuals as such, but of the whole body of the saved."[19] Hence, God foreknew a group. It is not individual persons but a group which God foreknew. God's foreknowledge is reduced from something personal to something impersonal.

In response, if it is argued God's foreknowledge is of a group, then we must also assume that the other actions of God, like the calling or justification, are likewise done to a group. Hence, groups are "called" or "justified" or "glorified." This simply does not square with the context. There are personal pronouns surrounding these verses. For example, the Spirit "helps *us* in our weakness," "intercedes *for us*"[20] (v. 26), "*we* know" (v. 28), and "*us*" (2x's, v. 31). Who are the "us" if not the Christians to whom Paul writes, including Paul himself? Indeed, in concluding his argument, Paul asks, "What then shall *we* say to these things? Since God is *for us*, who can be against *us*?" (v. 31, emphasis added) "These things" pertains to the fact that God foreknew, predestined, called, justified, and glorified his elect, which includes the Christians in Rome, many of whom Paul names in chapter 16, as well as Paul himself. It was Paul's intention that the golden chain of redemption have immediate application to the churches and individuals to whom he was writing. Therefore, this is not a nameless, faceless group which God foreknew. Rather, contra Coffman (and others), God foreknew (i.e., foreloved) from eternity individuals who then comprise the whole of the redeemed.

One more aspect of the Trinity's foreknowing and predestining work relates to the Father's relationship to the Son. Since the Son is "firstborn among many brothers," it seems reasonable that these many brothers are those whom the Father foreknew and predestined to be conformed to the Son. That is, those foreknown by the Father *just are* the many brothers of the Son. Since they are the Son's brothers, they are loved by the Father *even as* the Son is loved by the Father (John 17:23).

---

19. Coffman, "Commentary on Romans 8." These are his comments on Romans 8:28 and the phrase "called according to His purpose."

20. While the words "for us" (*huper hēmōn*, cf. e.g., v. 31) do not appear in this verse, the word Paul uses for "intercedes" (*huperentugchanei*) means to intercede on behalf of someone or for the sake of someone else (see Louw-Nida). Hence, the insertion of "for us" in most translations.

The Golden Chain of Redemption

Identifying the Call—General or Effectual?

Without doubt, the gospel is the means whereby God calls individuals, and the gospel is preached to all people. There is a general call which goes out to all people (e.g., Matt 22:14; Cf. Luke 14:16). Paul does not have that meaning here when he writes of "those whom [God] called." Paul is "called to be an apostle" (1:1), and these Christians in Rome are "called to be saints" (1:7). Further, in the immediate context, those whom God "called" in verse 30 are the same ones "called according to His purpose" in verse 28. In view is the effectual call of God's elect. Since this calling has in view those foreknown, predestined, justified, and glorified, it must be the call of God through the gospel to his elect made effectual by the powerful working of the Holy Spirit.

Further comparison and contrast between the general call and the effectual call (sometimes labeled external call and internal call respectively) can be demonstrated. Both are from God by means of the word. Both contain the same content (gospel). Both come to human beings who by nature are fallen sinners, children of wrath. Yet they are distinct. The general or external call is a call for people to repent and believe the gospel. It operates only by means of the word and the common grace operation of the Holy Spirit to bring conviction of sin. However, because of a person's condition as a fallen sinner and the effects of sin upon the mind, will, and heart, they refuse to repent and believe in Christ. Christ is undesirable to them, they reject the invitation, they make excuses, and prefer to continue doing things their way.

It must be noted that while the call of God certainly has gone into the world, it has not gone to *all* the world. That is, not every single person who has ever lived has heard the gospel. This is a fact so plain that it hardly needs defense. Only Abraham, himself an idolator (Josh 24:15), was called by God (Isa 51:2) and had the gospel preached to him (Gal 3:8). In addition, it was Abraham's seed, and no other nation, that God called out of Egypt (Deut 4:32–34). The testimony of the Old Testament is that while God has declared his word in Jacob, "He has not dealt thus with any other nation" (Ps 147:19–20). The same is true under the New Testament: while the call of the gospel has gone forth into entire areas, nations, people groups and languages, and resulted in God calling and Christ ransoming the elect "from every tribe, language, people, and nation" (Rev 5:9), not every single person who has ever lived on this side of the cross has had opportunity to hear (let alone respond to) the gospel. We in America ought to appreciate the fact

Part IV: Redemption Glorified

that the call of the gospel was not heard on this continent for hundreds of years! Hence, while the call of God through the gospel is general, it is not universal in the sense of reaching every single person who has ever lived.

Then there are those instances where the call of the gospel penetrates the very heart of a person. God, by means of the Holy Spirit and the word, powerfully and graciously works in a person's heart, mind, and will to grant them faith and repentance. God takes out the heart of stone and puts in a heart of flesh (Ezek 36:26). He calls a person out of darkness into light (1 Pet 2:9), thereby enlightening the mind (cf. Eph 1:18). The person unwilling to follow Christ is now made willing to follow him (cf. Ezek 36:27). That is, the Lord opens a person's heart so that they pay attention to the word of God (cf. Acts 16:14).

Coffman also confuses God's call of his elect with the general call of the gospel sometimes spoken of in Scripture. Like so many, he flattens the two calls into a single call. Then, he generalizes the target audience of the call to the body of Christ or the church as a whole. He then places the effectiveness of the calling upon the human individual. He assumes human capability to respond positively to the call as well as the ability of the individual to remain in a called state. He writes:

> Paul here did not speak of individuals as such, but of the whole body of the saved. That body, composed of the whole number of the redeemed, is indeed called and foreordained to eternal glory; but of an individual person, it must be said that he is called from before all time and predestinated to everlasting life, only if his affirmative response to the divine call has brought him into union with Christ, and if he so continues.[21]

A few sentences later he quotes from Lard who further generalizes by arguing that to be "called according to purpose" "is to be called according to the gospel."[22] So according to Lard and Coffman, "called" in Rom 8:30 is the general call of the gospel.

While it has been dealt with already, it bears repeating that Paul had individuals in mind, including himself, in this context. First person plural pronouns ("we," "us," "our") are used throughout (vs. 26, 28, 31, 32, et al). "The whole number of the redeemed" is composed of all those individuals whom God foreknew, predestined, called, justified, and glorified. Moreover, such a general call as Lard and Coffman present de-personalizes the

21. Coffman, "Commentary on Romans 8."
22. Coffman, "Commentary on Romans 8."

argument and takes away the intended applicational emphasis intended by the apostle for the church in Rome. This was not an exercise in theoretical redemption for Paul. He intends to drive home a message with immediate application for the Christians to whom he writes (viz., Rom 8:31ff).

When Paul writes of "those whom [God] called," he is writing of those who have heard the gospel and had the Holy Spirit powerfully work in them so that they are enabled to render an "affirmative response." This is the crucial difference between what Coffman (and Lard) presents and the divine perspective as presented by Paul in Rom 8:29–30: does our action enable God to do his work or does God's powerful working enable us to respond? Coffman (and many within and without the Restoration Movement), as seen from his commentary, argues for the former. Paul, though, only speaks of the latter ("He called"). This effectual call of God leads inexorably to the justification and glorification of Christ's "many brothers" (v. 29) who just are "God's elect" (v. 33). The call results in justification. Those called are those justified in this verse.

The gospel goes out into all the world. The prolific preaching of the gospel is the general call of the gospel. Sinners everywhere hear the gospel. For some, though, the gospel comes to them "only in word" (1 Thess 1:5). But for others, for those whom the Father foreknew and predestined to be conformed to the image of his Son, the gospel comes not only in word, "but also in power and in the Holy Spirit and with full conviction" (1 Thess 1:5). It is this powerful working of the Holy Spirit to convict and convert the sinner, to move them from unbelief to faith, which is the effectual call. These are those whom God called.

Glorified in the Aorist Tense

Attention has been given to Paul's use of the aorist tense for the final divine action in the golden chain of redemption: "He glorified." Below a couple specific arguments based on the aorist will be closely evaluated. Here general considerations concerning "He glorified" are presented. Kruse suggests three ways in which Paul's use of the aorist "He glorified" has been explained. One explanation is that Paul is communicating the certainty of glorification; it is as certain as predestination, calling, and justification. Since the glorification of believers is based on the divine decree, though it is yet to be realized at the end of time, it will be accomplished. Another explanation is to appeal to 2 Cor 3:18 and argue that the process of glorification

Part IV: Redemption Glorified

has begun in believers, though it will be completed at the return of Christ. The third way of explaining Paul's use of the aorist is to recognize that the kind of action is primarily in view, not the time of the action. Although the aorist typically refers to past action, it can be used to describe actions complete in themselves irrespective of time (i.e., past, present, or future).[23]

Of these options, the second option seems the weakest. It makes appeal to a verse outside the immediate context. It also overlooks previous usage of the aorist within the context of Rom 8 in relation to eschatological glorification. Two aorist tense verbs are used in verses 17 and 18 to describe the glorification of believers ("glorified with Him . . . glory to be revealed"). That these aorist tense verbs refer to future glory is evident since Paul specifically mentions the believers present suffering with Christ ("we suffer with Him," present tense) as well as contrasts the glory to be revealed with "the sufferings of this present time." These statements about our present sufferings juxtaposed with statements of glory that are clearly future from the context demonstrates that although the aorist tense is used, it has meaning beyond merely past tense.

The first and third options seem most plausible and perhaps can be combined. God's decree is in view since God's "purpose" is mentioned in verse 28. Moreover, what God decrees (or purposes) on behalf of believers is certain to come to pass. In addition, Lenski offers the defense for the gnomic or timeless use of the aorist in his comments on Rom 8:30.[24] He couples this with Paul's use of the pronoun "those," which Lenski identifies as "all the saved down to the last one to the end of time."[25] Therefore, the aorist as used here carries a timeless aspect. As will be shown below, others have argued for a proleptic or futuristic use of the aorist here.[26] All of these grammatical considerations of the aorist justify Paul's use of it for "He glorified."

---

23. Kruse, *Romans*, 357–58.

24. Lenski, *Romans*, 563. He appeals to A. T. Robertson's *Grammar* (836–37) for justification for the gnomic or timeless aorist. In the gnomic aorist section, Robertson specifically cites Romans 8:30 and *edoxase* as an example.

25. Lenski, *Romans*, 563.

26. E.g., Wallace who includes Romans 8:30 and "He glorified" as an example of the proleptic or futuristic use of the aorist (*Greek Grammar*, 563–64).

The Golden Chain of Redemption

The Use of the Aorist Tense for "He Glorified"

Sometimes an appeal is made to the fact that the verb for "He glorified" is in the "past" tense. Thus, like justification, glorification is something which happened to the believer when they became a Christian (and in churches of Christ, the definitive moment for this is baptism). Since all of the verbs (foreknew, predestined, called, justified, and glorified) are in the "past" tense, glorified, like the rest, must belong to the past for the Christian. In other words, once a person obeyed the gospel and was added to Christ's church and God's family, that person was glorified.

In response, clearly, a lot of weight is placed on the tense of the verb. First, to label the tense of verb "He glorified" as "past" tense is simplistic. "He glorified" is the aorist tense. While the aorist is often taught as a snapshot event in the past, there is much more to the aorist than that. Writing on verbal aspect, especially with reference to the aorist tense, Fred Long notes that the aorist conveys "unspecified action" or undefined action. Furthermore, "*tense in Greek has more to do with kind of action than time of action.*"[27] In addition, Daniel Wallace agrees, "*Tense is that feature of the verb that indicates the speaker's presentation of the verbal action (or state) with reference to its aspect [i.e., kind of action] and, under certain circumstances, its time.*"[28] Hence, while the aorist indicative "usually indicates *past* time with reference to the time of speaking,"[29] the above argument runs into the error of saying too much about the temporal aspect of the aorist indicative when used in Rom 8:30, especially as it pertains to "He glorified."

More will be discussed about the use of the aorist shortly when dealing with the interpretation of this text by T. W. Brents below. With this quick grammar lesson one can now determine that although the aorist tense is used for "He glorified," the emphasis in the verb is on the action taken by God on behalf of his people *from his perspective*, which is what Paul is presenting in these verses. In other words, from God's perspective (since this is his work and purpose through and through), the glorification of those whom God foreknew, predestined, called, and justified is as good as done.

Even without the grammar lesson, one can still determine from the surrounding context that the glorification in view in verse 30 is eschatological. The context for this verse began in verse 18. Verse 17 mentioned

---

27. Long, *Kairos*, 93. Emphasis original.
28. Wallace, *Greek Grammar*, 496. Emphasis original.
29. Wallace, *Greek Grammar*, 555.

Part IV: Redemption Glorified

our being "glorified with Him," i.e., with Christ. Paul then picks up on the thread of glorification in verse 18: "For I consider that the sufferings of this present time are not worth comparing with the glory that is to be revealed to us." First, "to us" (*eis hēmas*) can be understood as either "to us" (ESV, NASB), "in us" (NIV, NKJV), or "for us." Second, related to verb tense, both "glorified with Him" in verse 17 and "to be revealed" in verse 18 are both aorist tense verbs.[30] However, I doubt any would argue that these actions are somehow in our past simply because of the verb tense. Third, context clearly points to the future for when the glorification and the revelation of that glory will take place. The phrase "this present time" refers to the here-and-now, putting the revelation of our glorification in the there-and-then, despite using aorist tense verbs to describe it. Therefore, it is reasonable to understand God's glorification of his saints in verse 30 as eschatological. Returning to this theme at the close of this section puts a nice cap on a context which began with considerations of the glorification of the saints.

The appeal to verbal tense (with a twist) has shown up in church of Christ publications. T. W. Brents crafted an ingenious way to avoid what he considered "Calvinistic" overtones in Rom 8:29–30. He argued that since "all the verbs are in the past tense, and express actions perfected at the time the apostle wrote . . . it can not [sic] apply to any who have lived since that time."[31] Indeed, he goes so far as to argue that "the passage does not embrace all the elect, but it also shows that it did not refer to the apostles."[32] He then proceeds to introduce Matt 27:52–53 and those many saints who were resurrected when the Lord died on the cross as being those to whom Rom 8:29–30 is referring.

While this explanation is quite clever at avoiding "Calvinism," it is exegetically unsound. First, linguistically, Brents is correct that the aorist indicative is used for all five verbs. However, what he fails to understand is that the aorist tense is not univocal. In fact, the time element is secondary to the kind of action (*Aktionsart*) expressed in the verb. Thus, in writing about Greek verb tenses generally, A. T. Robertson notes, "Even in the indicative the time element is subordinate to the kind of action expressed."[33] Specific to the aorist tense Wallace discusses seven different uses. Included in that discussion is the proleptic or futuristic aorist "used to describe an

---

30. In verse 17, *sundoxasthōmen* is aorist passive subjunctive; in verse 18, *apokalupsthēnai* is aorist passive infinitive.

31. Brents, *Gospel Plan of Salvation*, 43.

32. Brents, *Gospel Plan of Salvation*, 45.

33. Robertson, *Grammar*, 825.

The Golden Chain of Redemption

event that is not yet past as though it were already completed." He cites Rom 8:30 and the verb for "He glorified" as an example.[34]

One may go further: a survey of the use of the aorist indicative when God is the subject of the verb (or the implied subject) both in Romans and in the wider Pauline corpus further torpedoes Brents's argument. For example, when discussing the universal revelation of God's wrath to all people Paul writes, "God has shown [*ephanerōsen*] it to them" (Rom 1:19). Later, in discussing God's intention to show mercy to disobedient Jews by showing mercy to the gentiles, Paul writes, "God has consigned [*sunekleisen*] all to disobedience" (Rom 11:32). Only the former is cited by Brents, though only to quote it. Here, though, are two examples where the aorist indicative is used which I doubt Brents would argue *must* be "actions perfected at the time the apostle wrote." Is not God still showing "what can be known about God" to all people? I am confident that Brents would not say that the consignment of all to disobedience took place before Paul wrote. Hence, we see distinction in how to understand the aorist indicative in Romans.

Outside of the book of Romans the case is only strengthened for recognizing that when the aorist indicative is used time is a secondary concern. For example, Paul asks, "Has not God made foolish [*emōranen*] the wisdom of the world?" (1 Cor 1:20) Was God's action of making the wisdom of the world foolish reserved only for the past prior to Paul? In addition, Paul affirms, "The Lord knows [*egnō*] those who are His" (2 Tim 2:19). Would Brents suggest that God only knew his own people prior to Paul? (Given Brents's view of God's knowledge, he might have.) Or should we not understand this as Paul stating the fact of God's comprehensive knowledge of his own people viewed as a single, complete action? Consider also what Paul writes concerning Jewish opponents who hindered him from preaching the gospel to gentiles: "But wrath has come upon [*ephthasen*] them at last!" (1 Thess 2:16) This clearly has an eschatological (futuristic) sense to it.[35] The aorist indicative is much more versatile than Brents acknowledges (and perhaps even realized). Thus, on linguistic grounds alone Brents's explanation of Rom 8:29–30 is erroneous.

Brents' explanation of Rom 8:29–30 is further wrong on exegetical grounds. For his explanation to work he must import Matt 27:52–53, concerning saints raised when Jesus died, into Rom 8:29–30. He argues that

---

34. Wallace, *Greek Grammar*, 563–64.

35. In fact, Wallace includes it as a possible example of the proleptic or futuristic aorist (*Greek Grammar*, 564).

Part IV: Redemption Glorified

these are the saints whom God foreknew, predestined, called, justified, and glorified. Are we to assume that not only did the church at Rome have a copy of the gospel of Matthew (which may be impossible given conventional dates for each document), but they would have also connected what Paul writes in 8:29–30 to what Matthew writes in 27:52–53? Such reasoning is simply incredulous.

Breaking the Golden Chain

The foregoing are examples at breaking the golden chain of redemption in one way or another. Each attempts to break the chain of redemption by introducing distinctions into the text which do not exist. One additional example occurs when a division is introduced between those called and those justified. "Predestined" and "called" are universalized to include all people; then, "justified" and "glorified" are limited to the redeemed. This is how Coffman reads Rom 8:29–30:

> The predestined include all people, although many refuse their destiny: the called include all people, although many shall not heed it; the justified are they alone who through the obedience of faith are transferred into Christ, in whom alone justification is possible; and the glorified are those finally redeemed above.[36]

In response, first, Coffman left out a key aspect of the golden chain of redemption, the first link in fact: those whom God foreknew. As discussed above, in this context, those whom God foreknew are his people. To then universalize "those whom He predestined" to include "all people," as Coffman does, is simply eisegetical. Context limits "those" (*hous*) to "the saints" (v. 27), Christ's "many brothers" (v. 29) and "God's elect" (v. 32), i.e., the "we" and "us" of this entire section. God's elect are the objects of the divine actions "foreknew" and "predestined," indeed, of all the actions in these verses (viz., "called," "justified," "glorified"). Coffman breaks the golden chain asunder!

Attempts to break the golden chain of redemption introduce categories and distinctions that are foreign to the text and context. God is the agent taking every action in Rom 8:29–30. Human choice and action are simply not present. The same objects receive each divine action in every instance, viz., the elect. There is no reason to introduce division between the links of this chain of redemption.

---

36. Coffman, "Commentary on Romans 8."

CHAPTER 13

Behold His Glory

WHERE DOES ONE END such a sweeping survey of the work of the triune God from eternity to eternity? Back where we began:

> Father, I desire that they also, whom you have given me, *may be with me where I am, to see my glory* that you have given me because you loved me before the foundation of the world. (John 17:24)

Earlier in this book (chapter three), it was established from this text that there is a particular people, both as a unit and individually, who are given by the Father to the Son. The Father entrusts his people to his Son. It was also established that this giving of people by the Father to the Son took place "before the foundation of the world." Let's go further.

The ultimate end of the will of Christ is that those given to him by the Father "be with Me where I am, to see My glory." While someone might point to the subjunctive mood of the verbs "be" and "see," since they are contained in *hina* clauses, it can be understood as purpose or result.[1] Therefore, Jesus is not merely expressing wishful thinking or possibilities. His will

---

1. The subjunctive mood expresses potential or possible action (see Long, *Kairos*, 204.) However, when contained in a *hina* clause, it is a dependent subjunctive, and one use is to communicate purpose or result (Long, *Kairos*, 205; Wallace, *Greek Grammar*, 448, 471–73, 664.) Here in John 17:24, the two phrases "may be with me where I am" (*hina hopou eimi egō kakeinoi ōsin*) and "to see my glory" (*hina theōrōsin tēn doxan tēn emēn*) both begin with *hina* and contain verbs in the subjunctive mood (*ōsin* and *theōrōsin*).

is that those given by the Father to him be with him and see his glory. His will results in those given to him by the Father be with him and see his glory. This is the will of the Son, which is also the will of the triune God.

Christ is coming to the Father (v. 13) and will no longer be in the world (v. 11). Indeed, the risen Lord has ascended into heaven to the Father's right hand (Acts 1:9; cf. Heb 8:1). Therefore, to be with Christ is to be in glory. Christ's prayer to the Father, which is an expression of his will to his Father, is that those given to him by the Father before the foundation of the world, for whom he died on the cross, whom the Spirit has made alive in due time and sanctified throughout their life, that these same ones "be with Me" in the glory of heaven.

More than that, to be with Jesus means to see his glory. This is the same glory he had before he came into the world, indeed, "before the world existed" (v. 5). This is the glory of God the Son which was veiled during his time on earth but which he has once again fully assumed as a result of his triumphant ascension to the right hand of God. The saints will gaze upon the unveiled glory of Christ their Savior in the glory of heaven. "We will see Him as He is" (1 John 3:2).

Christ's will is that "those who will believe in Me through their word" (v. 20), who *just are* those given by the Father to the Son, "be with Me where I am, so that they may see My glory" (LSB). I asked back in chapter three, Can it really be imagined that the will of Christ would be unfulfilled? Preposterous! Therefore, there is coming a day when all the elect of God (those given by the Father to the Son who believe in him by the Spirit) will enter into the perfect and immediate presence of the glorified Christ. All of Christ will be present with us. All of our being will be in the very presence of Christ. There will be no flesh, no faults, no weakness, no imperfections—nothing at all will hinder our experience and enjoyment of the glory of Christ.

This prayer of Jesus is inter-Trinitarian communication concerning the glorification of those given by the Father to the Son. The will ("desire," *thelō*) of the Son, which he prays to the Father, is that those given to him by his Father be where he is in order to see his glory, the same glory given to him by his Father. This is the will, intention, desire of the Son. It is the eternal will of the Son since, as is seen in the previous verse, he was sent by his Father on behalf of those loved by the Father *just as* he loved his Son which *just is* eternal love. It is the saving will of the Son since he came into the world, having been sent by the Father, to lay down his life for those given to him by the Father (cf. John 10:17–18). His eternal, saving will is fixed on his people and their eternal glorification.

Once more the time-bending aspect of redemption is evident when it is remembered that Christ is praying on the night he is betrayed for those future disciples who will believe that were given to him by the Father "before the foundation of the world." Past, present, and future meet in this single verse, highlighting the transcendent nature of the eternal purpose of God.

"To see My glory" is the intention of the Son for all those given to him by the Father. Heaven and eternity with him are the where and when of fulfillment of this intention. In heaven, and in our own glorified state, we will behold the glory of Christ. In heaven, when we are with him, we will see his glorious presence. In heaven, when we are where he is, we will behold the unveiled brilliance of his glory.

It is all those given by the Father to the Son—both those who were with him during his ministry as well as those who would believe through the word of the apostles—who will be with Jesus and see his glory. The Father gives these to the Son because he trusts the Son will accomplish all his will on their behalf (cf. John 6:38). In addition, the Father entrusts his people to the Son "because You loved Me." The Father has eternally loved the Son, evidenced by the timestamp "before the foundation of the world." This eternal inter-Trinitarian love is the basis and grounds for the hope of all who believe in Christ. The Father's love for the Son is the singular reason why he has given people to the Son. If one should wonder, "Why does He love me?" know that it is because the Father loves the Son.

Heaven is a world of love because heaven is the realm of the supreme manifestation of the love the triune God has for himself. In other words, heaven is where the Father, the Son, and the Holy Spirit express fully their eternal love for one another. To cite Edwards again, "There dwell God the Father, God the Son, and God the Spirit, united as one in infinitely dear, incomprehensible, mutual, and eternal love.[2]" That there exists an eternal love between the persons of the Trinity is evident in Jesus' words: "You loved Me before the foundation of the world." Jesus, God the Son incarnate, is speaking here to his Father in prayer. The Son says, "You [i.e., the Father] loved Me [i.e., the Son]." Such love that the Father has for the Son is beyond human comprehension since this is the love of one eternal person to another. This is the highest form of love: God the Father loves God the Son, or

---

2. Edwards, *Heaven*, 36.

Part IV: Redemption Glorified

God loves God. Moreover, the Father loved the Son "before the foundation of the world." Before the triune God set forth to work in creating the universe, they existed within a loving relationship one for the other. Such love transcends time and space. It is unfathomable. This is why heaven itself is a realm of love, even the love of the Father for his Son.

This prayer of Christ encompasses all time and stretches from eternity to eternity. It encapsulates the gospel from the divine perspective. The gospel begins and ends with the triune God. Therefore, herein is the gospel according to the Trinity.

CHAPTER 14

Putting It All Together

THE WORK OF THE Trinity is single and harmonious. All three persons work in concert with one another to accomplish their primary goal of mutual self-glorification in bringing many children to glory. There is inherent unity and harmony within the Trinity in this glorious work. However, how this is typically explained actually introduces disharmony and discord among the three persons of the Godhead. Nevertheless, Scripture affirms God's work in redemption is one work.

The biblical data is sufficient to conclude that in the triune God, as he has revealed himself, the three persons perform different roles in accomplishing their singular work of redemption: the Father elects, the Son dies, and the Holy Spirit sanctifies.[1] The glorious work of redemption performed by the Trinity is done to people. But does the work of the Trinity in redemption cohere as it is worked out on people? That is, is there agreement within the Trinity concerning their work in humans?

---

1. I am deliberately avoiding using terminology like "immanent Trinity" and "economic Trinity" because of the inherent disadvantages in it, as discussed in Sanders (*Triune God*, 144–48). As Sanders points out, and following "Rahner's Rule," the immanent Trinity *just is* the economic Trinity. Or, following Athanasius, as summarized by Torrance, "God is eternally and unchangeably Father, Son and Holy Spirit, three divine Persons who, while always Father, Son and Holy Spirit, in their co-indwelling and interpenetrating relations *are the Triune God*" (Torrance, *Trinitarian Faith*, 313. Emphasis original).

Part IV: Redemption Glorified

Three options arise concerning the scope of the work of redemption as it relates to humans: God redeems all people, some people, or no people. Given that there are three persons of the Godhead and three possible options as to the scope of the work each respective person of the Trinity is involved in, a total of twenty-seven possible outcomes result seen in the table below:

The Father Elects	None	None	None	None	None	None	None	None	None
The Son Dies For	None	None	None	Some	Some	Some	All	All	All
The Spirit Sanctifies	None	Some	All	None	Some	All	None	Some	All
The Father Elects	All	All	All	All	All	All	All	All	All
The Son Dies For	All	All	All	Some	Some	Some	None	None	None
The Spirit Sanctifies	All	Some	None	All	Some	None	All	Some	None
The Father Elects	Some	Some	Some	Some	Some	Some	Some	Some	Some
The Son Dies For	Some	Some	Some	None	None	None	All	All	All
The Spirit Sanctifies	Some	None	All	All	Some	None	All	Some	None

Table 1—Comparison of various possibilities of outworking of redemption

As can be seen by a cursory glance, most schemes for redemption postulate disharmony in the work of the Trinity. Many are outright unbiblical and even heretical. Some are uniquely absurd. Each option will be worked through in order to determine if it coheres with Scripture or not. For the sake of order, this study will classify the twenty-seven views under three major headings related to the Father's work of election: (1) the Father elects none, (2) the Father elects all, and (3) the Father elects some.

ERASING OR ELIMINATING ELECTION

The following nine options revolve around a denial or at least a downplaying of the Father's work in election. These begin with a failure to properly recognize the doctrine of election. Since the doctrine of election is a biblical doctrine, denial of it or failure to acknowledge it already sets these options at the severe disadvantage of not aligning with Scripture. Further considerations will likewise expose the fault in eliminating the Father's electing work.

Putting It All Together

The Father Elects None, the Son Dies for None, the Spirit Sanctifies None

The Father chooses no one in Christ, the Son dies for no one on the cross, and the Holy Spirit applies that work to no one. This is one of only three possibilities which has harmony within the Trinity. Clearly, though, this scheme would redeem no one. There is no redemption according to this model. No one is chosen by the Father. The Son dies for no one's sins and in no one's place. The Spirit, with no completed work to apply, does not apply the work because he cannot apply the work since it was never done. So while one ends up with harmony within the Trinity according to this model, it is nevertheless wholly unbiblical on all three counts of election, atonement, and sanctification. It is rejected.

The Father Elects None, the Son Dies for None, the Spirit Sanctifies Some

The Father chooses no one in Christ. The Son dies for no one on the cross. But the Holy Spirit applies the work of Christ to certain individuals. Immediately, the problem with this view is clear: the Spirit does not have the resources to accomplish his work of sanctification since the Son dies for no one. There can be no application of the work of Christ since that work was never done. Further, this is a disharmonious view. The Father and the Son are in agreement in that the audience for their work is the same: no one. However, the Holy Spirit is the rogue agent who is attempting to apply a non-existent work to certain people. Hence, the Spirit is opposed to the intentions of the Father and the Son. This model is rejected.

The Father Elects None, the Son Dies for None, the Spirit Sanctifies All

This view falls prey to the same factors as the previous option but to a greater degree. The Spirit is attempting to apply a non-existent work to everyone. However, since the Son dies for no one, it is not possible for the Spirit to then apply that unaccomplished work to all people. Also, assuming it were possible for the Spirit to accomplish his work independent of the other two persons of the Godhead, this would be universalism, all people being sanctified or made holy. However, universalism is unbiblical since there will be those who are ultimately lost. Further, this is a disharmonious view since, as mentioned, the Spirit is opposed to the intentions of the Father and the Son. This model is therefore rejected.

The Father Elects None, the Son Dies for Some, the Spirit Sanctifies None

The Father chooses no one in Christ, and the Son dies for certain individuals on the cross, but the Spirit does not apply Christ's completed work to any. According to this view, Christ dies for some people. Why these people? Absent the doctrine of election, which this view denies (the Father elects none), there is no definitive answer. Moreover, while Christ dies for certain people, the Spirit never applies his work to anyone. No one is saved since none have Christ's redemptive work applied to them. Finally, this view is disharmonious. The Son is the rogue agent who dies for certain individuals in opposition to the intentions of the Father and the Spirit. This view is rejected.

The Father Elects None, the Son Dies for All, the Spirit Sanctifies None

This view suffers from the same problems as the previous possibility but to a greater extent. The Son dies for everyone everywhere, a view of the atonement held my most people today. However, the doctrine of election and sanctification are absent. Therefore, while the resources are available to redeem the whole world, the Spirit never applies the completed work of Christ to anyone. Once more, this view presents disharmony among the Godhead, with the Son dying for all in opposition to the intentions of the Father and the Spirit. As a result, this view is rejected.

The Father Elects None, the Son Dies for Some, the Spirit Sanctifies Some

The Father chooses no one, yet the Son dies for certain individuals on the cross, and the Spirit applies that completed work to certain individuals. Since the Father elects no one, there is no doctrine of election. One is left to wonder, "Why redeem and sanctify these individuals?" As seen before, without a doctrine of election there can be definitive answer to this question. Further, those for whom the Son dies would seemingly be those whom the Spirit sanctifies. However, there is no guarantee this is the case since the Trinity is not united in intent and purpose according to this view. The Son and the Spirit are operating independent of the intentions of the Father. Again, this is a disharmonious view of the work of the Trinity. It is rejected.

The Father Elects None, the Son Dies for All, the Spirit Sanctifies Some

According to this outworking of redemption, the Father chooses no one in particular. The Father then sends the Son into the world to die for all people. Then, the Father and the Son send the Spirit to set apart some people for God. This may be a contender for a view of redemption within Restoration Movement churches and perhaps not a few evangelical churches.

It is possible that the doctrine of election is not erased entirely in this view. Rather, it is reduced from a personal choice by the Father to an impersonal one: the Father chose *to save* or he chose a plan. Thus, the Father sends the Son to provide a *potential* salvation for all people, and the Spirit is sent to apply that work to "whosoever will."

There are glaring issues with this account. First, the view of election offered does not square with the biblical witness. As established, the Father "chose us in Him" (Eph 1:4). It is people ("us"), not a plan or purpose, which the Father chose. Moreover, as argued elsewhere, if Jesus dies for all, which according to Scripture means he substitutes in their place and for their sins, then their sins are covered and forgiven. Thus, if he does that for all, then the sins of every last God-hating rebel, including Pharaoh, the Amorite high priest in the Old Testament, and Nero and Domitian, are taken away, forgiven. Jesus has borne their sins which means they are not under their sins. God has punished their sins in Christ on the cross. But if this is the case, no sinner should be facing a devil's hell since Jesus bore their sins in his body on the tree.

The Spirit has abundant resources since Christ died for all according to this view. However, he only applies the completed work of Christ—a work completed for each and every person ever—to certain individuals. Since there is not a doctrine of personal election, there is no definitive theocentric answer as to why Christ accomplishes redemption for each and every person ever, but the Spirit only applies that completed work to certain individuals. Instead, what is required is an accounting for human autonomy or libertarian free will whereby people choose God.

Further, this is a disharmonious view which presents all three persons of the Trinity at odds with one another. Their intentions are at cross purposes, which means their actions are also out of sync. The Father acts in a certain way for no one, while the Son acts a certain way for everyone, and the Spirit acts a certain way to certain people. Hence, according to this view, the work of the Trinity is three and disharmonious. While this view may be popular among many Christians, it is theologically insufficient and biblically wanting. It is rejected.

The Father Elects None, the Son Dies for All, the Spirit Sanctifies All

The Father chooses no one, yet the Son dies for all people, and the Spirit applies that completed work to everyone. According to this model, the Son dies for every single person ever. Then, the Spirit, sent by the Father and the Son, applies that work to every single person ever. Hence, everyone is saved without reference to the Father. Absent the doctrine of election, one wonders why the Son and the Spirit are redeeming everyone.

This view suffers from universalist tendencies as well. Like the previous view, Jesus dies for the sins of and in the place of each and every person ever. The wrath for their sins is fully satisfied. This view goes further and argues that the Spirit then applies the completed work of Christ to each and every person ever. Every single person, including Pharaoh and the Amorite high priest, are made holy. Therefore, no one faces a devil's hell. However, this does not square with the biblical data that there will be those who are ultimately lost.

Finally, this view introduces disharmony into the Trinity. While the Son and the Spirit are in full agreement with one another as to the work of redemption, they are out of sync with the Father's work in election. Once again the Son and the Spirit are operating independent of the Father. It could be said that they are doing their work "of themselves" without reference to the Father. This being the case, this model is rejected.

Putting It All Together

The Father Elects None, the Son Dies for Some, the Spirit Sanctifies All

The Father chooses no one from eternity. Then, the Father sends the Son to die for some people. Finally, the Father and the Son send the Spirit to sanctify every single person ever. Such a chaotic scheme immediately betrays the disharmony this view introduces into the Trinity. Further, there is a tinge of universalism in the Spirit's work. Disharmonious universalism results from this view.

Here the resources necessary for the Spirit to accomplish his work of sanctifying all people are insufficient since the Son's atonement is intended for only some people. The Spirit ends up sanctifying everybody. Further, without the doctrine of election, one wonders, "Why is the Son dying for some of humanity?" Who are those for whom Christ dies if the Father has not freely chosen his people? The Father, the Son, and the Holy Spirit are at odds with one another, each one doing very different actions in the work of redemption. This disharmonious view is rejected.

Summary

None of these possibilities satisfies the biblical data concerning the triune God's work of redemption. Absent the doctrine of election, in views which have the Son and the Spirit actually working redemption in humanity, whether universally or particularly, one wonders, "Why are the Son and the Spirit doing what they are doing?" In addition, without the Father's work in election, there exists disharmony within the Godhead. Disharmonious views ought to be summarily rejected. The only harmonious view under this heading is wholly unbiblical. Therefore, we must look elsewhere for the biblical model for the triune God's work of redemption.

HYPER-ELECTION

This section is classified "Hyper-election" in order to label the notion that the Father elects all. If the Father elects all, that *just is* the Father saving all. Hence, this final section has universalist overtones. Universalism is "the notion that all intelligent, moral creatures (angels, humans, devils) will be saved in the end."[2] While this is the doctrine proper, typically what is meant is the salvation of all human beings. While outside the scope of this work, Universalism can be demonstrated as erroneous.[3] Further examination of each view respectively will further show the error of universalizing the Father's work in election.

The Father Elects All, the Son Dies for All, the Spirit Sanctifies All

On the one hand, this view benefits from being one of the three harmonious views. All three persons of the Trinity are at work for the same lot of humanity, viz., everyone. Their intention is singular and united. On the other hand, this is universalism. All people are elect. All sins are forgiven in Christ's death. All are regenerated and sanctified. However, none of this reflects the biblical text.

It is possible that this could be a contender for Karl Barth's revisioning of the electing work of God. According to a Barthian view, the Father's work of election is centered on his choosing of the Son. The Father does not choose people; the Son is the elect one. Barth writes, "In its simplest and most comprehensive form the dogma of predestination consists, then, in the assertion that the divine predestination is the election of Jesus Christ."[4] Christ, then, is both the electing God and the elected man.[5] Barth's doctrine of election also had a universalist flavor to it since the "object and content" of divine election is "the salvation of all men."[6] While Barth's revision of election is intriguing, and perhaps has basis in the biblical witness (Christ is the Father's "Chosen One," Luke 9:35), since the work of redemption by the triune God is worked out in humanity, such theological and Christological considerations, while noteworthy, are beyond the scope of this work.[7]

---

2. Gundry-Volf, "Universalism," 956.

3. See Appendix—Universalism.

4. *CD*, II.2:103.

5. For a summary of Barth's doctrine of election, see Allen, *Karl Barth's Church Dogmatics*, 71–72; Van Til, *Christianity and Barthianism*, 34–42.

6. Van Til, *Christianity and Barthianism*, 116.

7. For a critique of Barth's doctrine of election see Van Til, *Christianity and Barthianism*, 160–71. Specifically, Van Til presents the critical work of three authors (Idema, Trimp, and Berkouwer): "Barth's view of election in Christ is no election at all, for it pertains universally to man as man" (163); "The Christ of Barth, if he may be said to save any man at all, saves all men to participation in himself" (166); "Barth's view of election, and with it that of sin, may be said to involve the Christological goodness of

We will pass it by once more noting that Paul wrote, "[God] chose *us* in [Christ]" (Eph 1:4). As demonstrated throughout this work, the doctrine of election is personal; God chose people.

Whether or not this view reflects Barth accurately, it does not fit with the biblical record. First, the Father "chose us in Him"; it does not say the Father "chose all in Him." Election is personal and specific, not universal and indiscriminate. Second, and related to the first, while Christ is the Father's chosen one (i.e., the elect one), he lays down his life for all those given to him by the Father (i.e., the elect). Third, he participates as himself (i.e., God the Son) in the work of election with the Father (cf. John 13:18) and therefore knows all those whom he has chosen. Fourth, while universal atonement advocates are happy with the Son dying for all, since Christ's death on the cross actually accomplishes redemption, a universal atonement would amount to universal salvation (i.e., universalism). Moreover, the application of Christ's atoning work by the Spirit would also equate with universalism. However, Scripture affirms that the benefits of his death are not applied to all by the Spirit. So this view falls short of what Scripture teaches concerning the work of the triune God in redemption. Therefore, this view is rejected.

The Father Elects All, the Son Dies for All, the Spirit Sanctifies None

The Father chose all people to be redeemed. He then sends the Son to die on the cross for all people. However, the Spirit does not apply that completed work to any people. All are chosen and atoned for, but none are actually sanctified. The absurdity of this view ought to be self-evident: despite having all the resources necessary to accomplish his work in redemption, the Spirit fails to perfectly apply that work to any person. Further, as with the overwhelming majority of these various models, this one suffers from inter-Trinitarian disharmony, the Spirit at cross purposes with the Father and the Son. This absurdity and disharmony result in the rejection of this model.

---

human nature" (169–70); and "Even the idea of substitutionary atonement comes to be an emptied matter on Barth's view of election" (170). See also Scheurers, "Evaluation of Some Aspects," 161–73.

Part IV: Redemption Glorified

The Father elects all, the Son Dies for None, the Spirit Sanctifies All

In this model the Father chose all people to be redeemed. However, the Son, sent by the Father, dies on the cross for no one. The Spirit then works to sanctify everyone. Immediately, the Trinitarian disharmony is evident. The Father and the Spirit are in union, but the Son's work is out of sync with them. This results in the Spirit lacking the resources necessary to accomplish his sanctifying work. There is no work of Christ to apply. Furthermore, the unbiblical nature of this model is clear since Christ died for sinners (Rom 5:8). This model denies this biblical truth. Therefore, this model is rejected.

The Father Elects all, the Son Dies for None, the Spirit Sanctifies Some

This model is nearly identical to the previous model. The only difference is the proposed scope of the Spirit's work: from all to some. The same problematic issues plague this model as the previous: Trinitarian disharmony, the Spirit lacking resources to accomplish his work (despite the target audience being smaller), and the unbiblical proposal for the Son's work on the cross. This model is to be rejected.

The Father Elects All, the Son Dies for Some, the Spirit Sanctifies None

Once again, the Father chose all people to be redeemed. The Son dies for some people. The Spirit, though, applies that completed work to no one. Immediately, Trinitarian disharmony is evident as all three persons of the Godhead are functioning very differently in the work of redemption. It is the Father's will, according to this view, that all be redeemed. The Son, though, dies only for certain individuals. In other words, the Son fails to accomplish the will of the Father. However, this is unbiblical since the Son came to do the will of him who sent him (John 6:38). Such disobedience would be the undoing of the Godhead!

The problem is further compounded when one considers that while Christ dies for certain people, the Spirit never applies his work to anyone. No one is saved since none have Christ's redemptive work applied to them. The Spirit, in similar manner, fails to accomplish the will of the Father. Again, such disobedience would mean the end of the Godhead.

Trinitarian disharmony runs amok with this view. Each of the three persons of the Trinity are operating "of Himself" without reference to the other two. Furthermore, the unbiblical aspects of this view—the disobedience of the Son and no one being saved—means it is rejected.

The Father Elects All, the Son Dies for Some, the Spirit Sanctifies Some

In this view, the Father chose everyone to be redeemed. The Son, though, dies on the cross for only some of humanity. The Spirit then applies the work of the Son to those for whom he died. As with the previous view, this view suffers from the Son being disobedient to the Father. Furthermore, there is disharmony within the Trinity since the Son and the Spirit, while in agreement, are at odds with the Father. Given these glaring faults, this view is rejected.

The Father Elects All, the Son Dies for Some, the Spirit Sanctifies All

Once more, the Father chose all people for redemption. However, the Son dies on the cross only for certain people. The Spirit then applies this work to all people. Yet again, this model is subject, like so many, to the charge of disharmony within the Trinity. The Son is out of sync with the other two persons of the Godhead. Further, the Spirit lacks the resources necessary to do his work since the Son dies for some, not for all. This view also has shades of universalism to it, and universalism is unbiblical. These considerations eliminate this model.

The Father Elects All, the Son Dies for All, the Spirit Sanctifies Some

Here is perhaps another contender for a possible scheme for redemption among the Restoration Movement and perhaps many evangelicals. The Father elects for everyone to be saved (sometimes it may be presented as "The Father has cast His vote, and the devil has cast his vote. Now you get to cast the deciding vote."). The Son is sent by the Father to die for all people. Then, the Spirit, sent by the Father and the Son, applies the finished work of Christ to some individuals, setting them apart for God.

According to this outworking, election is universalized and reduced to mere desire. It is not that the Father chooses people as much as he merely *wants* all people to be saved and is doing all he can to save everybody. The Father's efforts at saving everybody culminates in sending the Son to die for all on the cross. Salvation is made possible, though it remains hypothetical until a person decides for Jesus. Once a person decides for Jesus, then the Spirit applies Christ's completed work to them.

In response it must be recognized that the work of the Father in election from eternity is not a mere desire or intention. Election is not wishful thinking on the Father's part. Election is actual and real. "Before the foundation of the world," the Father chose his beloved people in the Son. In addition, there is nothing hypothetical about the atonement. Like the Father's election, the Son's atonement is actual and real. This is why the gospel is in the indicative mood in the New Testament.

In addition, this view falls prey to the introduction of disharmony to the Trinity. The Father and the Son are in agreement in their respective works of election and atonement, but the Spirit acts independently of the other two persons. The Spirit works sanctification "from Himself," only applying Christ's completed work to some people. Though these would be elect, it is not *all* God's elect. Hence, this view is rejected.

The Father Elects All, the Son Dies for None, the Spirit Sanctifies None

The Father chooses all people for redemption. He then sends the Son into the world to die on the cross for no one. Then, the Spirit is sent by the Father and the Son to set apart no one. Immediately it is plain that there is disharmony within the Trinity, the Father's will contrary to that of the Son and the Spirit. Additionally, the works of the Son and the Spirit as represented in this view do not reflect what is found in Scripture. The Son died "for sins," i.e., the sins of people (1 Pet 3:18). If he dies for no one, he does not die for sins. Moreover, people, both Jews and gentiles, are "sanctified by the Holy Spirit" (Rom 15:16). Hence, this model is unbiblical and is rejected.

Summary

If any one person of the Trinity, while fulfilling their role in redemption, acts in a manner different than the other two persons of the Trinity, then disharmony is introduced into the Godhead. So the drift of the argument for Trinitarian harmony within the Godhead in the work of redemption is that if, for example, the Son offered himself for a people (or even a person) other than those given to him by the Father whom he has chosen to save and whom the Spirit himself would regenerate, then the Son would be out of step with the triune purpose.[8] But, as argued earlier in this work, such a thought is outside the realm of possibility, given the unity of intention and purpose which exists within the Trinity. Thus, for the Father to elect all for salvation but the Son and the Spirit fail in bringing all the elect to glory is a nonstarter. Once more one must look elsewhere for a biblical model of the triune God's work in redemption.

ELECTION IN FOCUS

When it comes to election, the fact from Scripture is that the Father has not chosen everybody in Christ—whether in time or before time (though Scripture affirms the latter as the "when"). The doctrine of the Father's kingly freedom in choosing or electing his people in the Son has been established elsewhere in this work. Therefore, it is biblical and reasonable to affirm the Father's kingly freedom in choosing his people from eternity.

Before time began, according to his wise and holy counsel, and for his own purpose, pleasure, and glory, God chose to save a certain number of sinners. His choice is not arbitrary because an ultimate being cannot be arbitrary ("all His ways are just," Deut 32:4 [LSB]). Nor is his choice based on "foreseen faith" or any goodness in fallen creatures (Eph 2:9; Titus 3:5). The basis for the choice of the triune God is found in God himself, whose wisdom and knowledge knows no bounds, his judgments unsearchable, and his ways impossible to comprehend (Rom 11:33).

There are those who object to such a doctrine. They find it distasteful that God could chose to have mercy on some and not on others. It is not fair that God exercises his kingly freedom in this way, despite the fact that the Bible presents God as doing just that. He says as much: "For [God] says to Moses, 'I will have mercy on whom I have mercy, and I will have compassion on whom I have compassion'" (Rom 9:15; cf. Exod 33:19). As others have pointed out, the verbs used here could be translated, "I mercy whom I mercy and I compassion whom I compassion" (though that makes for poor

---

8. Zaspel argues this is the thrust of Warfield's argument in *The Plan of Salvation*, though "Warfield does not quite say it in these words" (*Theology of B. B. Warfield*, 310).

Part IV: Redemption Glorified

English). So the kingly freedom (i.e., sovereignty) that so many balk at *just is* what is taught in their New Testament.

Restoration Movement folk have historically balked at the idea of God electing some from eternity and not others. Mostly the confusion stems from collapsing the eternal work of the triune God into the framework of history and time. Brents is typical; after citing Eph 2:3, he writes:

> If they had been elected to salvation before time began, we see not how, at any time, they could have been *children of wrath*, even as others not of the elect. [Cites Rom 8:9] All persons know that, prior to conversion, the Spirit of Christ was not in them, and hence, at that time, they were none of His; yet according to the theory [of eternal and unconditional election], they were *always* His. [Cites Rom 8:14] Then of course the converse is true, that as many as are not led by the Spirit of God are not the sons of God. All unconverted persons are led by the spirit of the wicked one, and not by the Spirit of God; therefore no unconverted man is a son of God. It will be conceded that the elect are sons of God; hence *when not sons of God, none are elect* . . . All the elect are Christ's; therefore there was a time in the life of every man when he was not of the elect: hence none are personally and unconditionally elected to eternal life from before the foundation of the world.[9]

First, Brents confuses several categories. He confuses time and eternity. He confuses election with conversion; election takes place in eternity (i.e., before time), while conversion takes place in time. He confuses God's election of his people in eternity with that people's status in time prior to and after conversion. He confuses our status according to the immutable decree of God and our status in time, which is mutable as God's sovereign purposes are worked out in due time. Therefore, this is a not a fair and accurate depiction of what Brents claims to be opposed to.

Second, Brents does not have a robust Trinitarian understanding of redemption.[10] This results in confusion on Brents's part since he assumes all that is required for redemption is the immutable decree of election by the Father. He fails to realize that included in the decree of God is the obedient sacrifice of the Son to ransom all his people and the Spirit's regenerating and sanctifying work.

---

9. Brents, *Gospel Plan of Salvation*, 36–37. Emphasis original.

10. Indeed, Brents denied the Trinity and was not shy about being anti-Trinitarian. In his sermon "The Sonship of Christ," Brents introduces the sermon by saying, "Neither Trinitarianism nor Unitarianism is true" (Brents, *Gospels Sermons*, 21).

Third, Brents fails to distinguish between the actions of the triune God in eternity and the actions of the triune God in time. What was determined in eternity is fulfilled in time (e.g., the death of the Son on the cross). Then, in due time, the blessings secured by Christ on the cross are applied to the elect by the Holy Spirit. Brents flattens all this together. As a result, he renders the eternal work of the Father null and void. Indeed, he makes election *our* work.

Fourth, the unbiblical nature of Brents's statement ought to be evident. Whereas Scripture says God chose us in Christ before the foundation of the world, Brents says such election did not take place. For Brents, election takes place in time at conversion by people.

Brents notwithstanding, what the sanctified heart marvels at is not that God chooses to have mercy on some but that he chose to have mercy on *anybody*! Humans are sinners worthy of divine justice and wrath due to our sins. Each person is clay in the hands of the potter for him to mold, shape, and use as he deems fit according to his kingly freedom (see Rom 9:19–24). As the old illustration goes, the same sun which melts the wax hardens the clay. Such a truth is repugnant to unregenerate people. At the same time, the clearest evidence of the work of true grace in the truly regenerate heart is when they love those aspects of God's character and his attributes which the natural man detests.

Since it is not all people, the Father's purpose of election is that from the whole lot of fallen humanity, the Father chose some ("us") in Christ Jesus, the Son. From this starting point, we are now ready to pursue the remainder of the possible options.

The Father Elects Some, the Son Dies for All, the Spirit Sanctifies Some

Here is another strong contender for Restoration Movement churches and perhaps many evangelical churches. The Father elects some to salvation in Christ. The Father then sends the Son into the world to die for all people. The Father and the Son send the Spirit into the world to then apply that work through sanctification to some people.

Immediately we recognize the disharmony of this view. The Father and the Spirit are at odds with the Son. The work the Father and the Spirit perform is on behalf of the elect, while the Son's work is on behalf of everyone. The Father chooses people whom he gives to the Son so that he might ransom them, only to have the Son come into the world and die for all people. Then, upon the return of the Son to the Father having done a work which was beyond the Father's intention, the Father and the Son send the Holy Spirit into the world to apply that work to all those chosen by the Father, all of whom were atoned for at the cross, but not all those for whom Christ died (i.e., the rest of humanity). Why does the Son disobey his Father and die for those not given to him?

The answer seems to be that most Christians have a sentimental or emotional view of the atonement rather than a biblical and theological view of the atonement. Many Christians look to the cross and only see love: Jesus loves everyone, and therefore Jesus dies for everyone. Such a view flattens the love of God so that there are no distinctions within it. Hence, the love Christ has for his enemies whom he puts under his feet and makes his footstool is the same love he has for those given to him by the Father. While it is true that there is a general or universal love that God has for all people, his redemptive love, called "His great love with which He loved us" (Eph 2:4), is different and reserved exclusively for his redeemed.

An illustration may help: as a Christian man, I am to love my enemies. However, I would be confused at best and outright sinful at worst to love my enemies *in the same way* that I love my children. Or as a Christian husband, I am to love my wife. But I would be dead wrong to love another man's wife *in the same way* as I love my wife. So we readily make distinctions when it comes to human love. Why does God not get to do the same with his love? Is God free to love whom he wills? Unfortunately, I believe many Christians would answer that question, "No." Or at least, "Yes, but, etc."

Such sentimentality has the wrong starting point. It starts below, with us and what we want, rather than starting above, with God and the divine intention of the Father, the Son, and the Holy Spirit. Further, such sentimentality also introduces confusion and disharmony to the Godhead, the Son working at cross purposes with the other two persons of the Godhead. The Son does not and cannot die for those whom the Father has not elected. Finally, this sentimental view of the cross runs counter to the biblical view of what Christ accomplished on the cross, as argued elsewhere in this book.

Putting It All Together

The Father Elects Some, the Son Dies for All, the Spirit Sanctifies None

The Father chooses some for redemption. He then sends his Son into the world to die on behalf of all people. The Father and the Son send the Holy Spirit, who actually sanctifies no one.

The disharmony of this view is evident since all three persons of the Godhead are all doing different things in relation to redemption. The Father, the Son, and the Holy Spirit are all at cross purposes with one another. Further, while the Son actually accomplishes redemption for all people (which, as argued elsewhere in this book, means all sinners with all their sins are really forgiven), none are actually saved since his completed work is never applied to any in sanctification. The blessings secured at the cross are never applied by the Spirit.

This may be a contender for a view within a certain branch of the Restoration Movement, viz., those who deny direct operation of the Holy Spirit. It checks the box for the universal atoning work of Christ prevalent among churches of Christ ("Christ died for all"). It also narrows the Spirit's work: he operates only through the word (cf. John 17:17). However, given our aversion to and (re)definition of election, it is a non-starter. The Father does not have the freedom to save whom *he* wills, but only *whosoever* wills. Furthermore, the Spirit fails in the work that was determined for him before the foundation of the world. Therefore, while it may marginally suit some within the Restoration Movement, it is to be rejected for the reasons given.

The Father Elects Some, the Son Dies for all, the Spirit Sanctifies All

The Father elects some people from among the lot of fallen humanity before time. Then, the Father sends the Son into history who dies on the cross for all people. Finally, the Father and the Son send the Holy Spirit into the world, who applies the completed work of Christ to all people.

Disharmony is yet again present in this view. The Son and the Spirit are united in their work but are at odds with the Father's intention from eternity in election. The Son and the Spirit go rogue in their work. In addition, universalism is another glaring failure of this view (assuming the Son and the Spirit can redeem all people, including those whom the Father did not choose). The application of the redemptive work of Christ by the Spirit necessarily results in salvation. Since Christ dies for every person ever and the Spirit applies that completed work to every person ever, every person ever will be saved. The unbiblical aspects of this view leads to its rejection.

The Father Elects Some, the Son Dies for None, the Spirit Sanctifies Some

According to this view, the Father chooses certain people from eternity. The Son is sent by the Father into the world to die on the cross, and although he dies, it effectively saves no one. Then, the Spirit is sent to sanctify in due time those chosen by the Father.

Like with so many other schemes, disharmony is present in this view. The Father and the Spirit are in agreement; however, the Son is out of sync with the other two persons of the Trinity. Further, the Son, though he dies, does not accomplish redemption. None are redeemed, even though the Father chose some.

In addition, according to this view, the atonement is rendered ineffectual in this view. Christ redeems no one. Are we to think that the Son would fail to effectively redeem his people? The Son does not fail to redeem all those given to him by the Father. Finally, the Spirit lacks the resources necessary to accomplish his work. While the Spirit is in agreement with the Father and intends to sanctify those chosen by the Father, the Son's sacrifice is ineffectual since he dies for no one in particular. Therefore, the Spirit cannot do his work in redemption. These reasons disqualify this view.

The Father Elects Some, the Son Dies for None, the Spirit Sanctifies All

In this model, the Father chooses his elect in eternity. The Father sends the Son into the world, and while the Son does die on the cross, it effectively redeems no one. Then, the Father and the Son send the Spirit into the world and he sanctifies all people.

Every person of the Trinity is operating in a disharmonious manner. Each of the three persons are working at counter purposes with the other persons. The Father chooses some, the Son dies for no one, but the Spirit sanctifies everyone. In addition, there are also universalistic overtones here, as the Spirit is sanctifying all people.

Are we to assume that the Spirit would sanctify more people than those chosen by the Father? The Spirit will not and cannot sanctify those whom the Father has not chosen. Like the previous view, this model also suffers from a lack of recourses for the Spirit, except to a greater degree. Since Christ dies on behalf of no one, he secures no blessings for any particular person. There is no completed work to apply, yet somehow the Spirit is sanctifying everyone. This model is to be rejected.

The Father Elects Some, the Son Dies for None, the Spirit Sanctifies None

In this view, the Father chooses his people from eternity. However, the Son dies for no one's sins and in no one's place. The Spirit, having no work to apply, sanctifies no one.

The disharmony inherent in this model is evident since the Spirit and the Son are in agreement but are opposed to the Father. In addition, as demonstrated earlier, this view is unbiblical since the Son, according to the Scriptures, does die for sins and for sinners. Furthermore, the Spirit really does sanctify the saints, which likewise accentuates the unbiblical aspects of this model.

Perhaps the biggest death blow to this model and those like it is that no one is saved. The Son dying for no one and the Spirit sanctifying no one results in no one being saved. Again, the disharmony is seen since from eternity the Father determined to save (via election) some. Likewise, the unbiblical nature of this view is also seen since Jesus is "the Savior of the world" (John 4:42; 1 John 4:14). But if he actually saves no one, he cannot be Savior of the world. Therefore, this model is to be rejected.

The Father Elects Some, the Son Dies for Some, the Spirit Sanctifies All

The Father chooses his people in Christ in eternity. Then, the Father sends the Son into the world, and he accomplishes the redemption of all those given to him by the Father. The Father and the Son send the Spirit into the world who applies Christ's completed work to everyone.

Like so many other models, this one suffers from disharmony within the Trinity. While the Father and the Son are united in their respective work (election and atonement), the Spirit is the rogue agent. In this model, the Father elects some and the Son dies for those chosen by the Father and given to him. However, the Spirit seeks to sanctify every single person ever. Such disharmony renders this model untenable.

Moreover, the Spirit does not have sufficient resources to do his work. The Son dies for those given to him by the Father and for those only. The Spirit, though, is attempting to take the blessings secured by the Son for the elect and apply them to all people. As Jesus has taught, the Spirit does not act "on His own authority" or "of Himself" (John 16:13). Thus, the Spirit will not do his work independent of the Father and the Son. There are also hints of universalism here since those whom the Spirit sanctifies will be saved. Based on these considerations this model is to be rejected.

The Father Elects Some, the Son Dies for Some, the Spirit Sanctifies None

This view is virtually identical with the previous view, with the difference being the Spirit's work: the Spirit sanctifies no one. This view suffers from the same problems as the previous as well but to a greater degree. Once again, there is disharmony within the triune God. While the Father and the Son agree in electing and redeeming a particular people, the Spirit fails to apply Christ's atoning work to anybody. As with other views, the Spirit goes rogue, operating independently from the Father and the Son.

According to this view, the Spirit fails in applying the Son's finished work in atonement and the Father's electing work. We are left to wonder, "Does the Spirit fail in His work of sanctification?" To ask the question is to answer it: absolutely not! The Spirit will not act "of Himself." Since this model sees the Spirit acting "of Himself," and it introduces disharmony within the Trinity, it is rejected.

The Father Elects Some, the Son Dies for Some, the Spirit Sanctifies Some

Here is the final view which honors Trinitarian harmony in the work of redemption. All three persons are united in their intention to glorify themselves in the salvation of a particular people. Hence, the Father chooses some in Christ before the foundation of the world. Then, the Father sends

Putting It All Together

the Son into the world to accomplish the redemption of those chosen in him. Finally, the Father and the Son send the Spirit into the world to perfectly apply the completed work of Christ to his people from every nation, language, tribe, and ethnic group throughout history. While this view is often labeled "Calvinistic," it is better recognized as the biblical view or at least the historic Christian faith.[11]

Each aspect of this view agrees with Scripture. It has been demonstrated in this work that the Father chose his people in Christ before time began. It has also been shown that the Son, sent by the Father, entered into his own creation as a human being and perfectly accomplished the redemption of those given to him by the Father. It has likewise been explained that the Spirit, sent by the Father and the Son, in due time perfectly applies the completed work of Christ in setting apart all God's elect.

Of course, a main objection to this view is, Why does God choose some and not others? As seen above, such an objection can be made to other views. This is by no means a problem exclusive to this view. Moreover, the answer to this question is supplied in Scripture. After stating the Father's election of a specific people in the Son from eternity whom he predestined to adoption in Christ, Paul adds that all this was "to the praise of His glorious grace" (1:6). This refrain is repeated in slightly different form in vs. 12 and 14: "to the praise of His glory." For his glory and grace to be praised by his people is the reason God chose, redeemed, and sanctified some sinners.

This echoes similar statements found elsewhere in Scripture. God forms a people "for Myself that they might declare My praise" (Isa 43:21). Those called by Yahweh's name are those "created for My glory" (Isa 43:11). God does what he does "for My own sake, for My own sake" (Isa 48:11). Yahweh has set apart the godly for himself (Ps 4:3). It is "for the glory of Your Name" and "for Your Name's sake" that God saves, delivers, and atones for sins (Ps 79:9). God acts in the way he acts because he is shown glorious, praiseworthy, and central to whatsoever happens. Everything is all about God. Therefore, when the question is asked, "Why does God choose, redeem, and sanctify some but not others?" the answer God himself gives is "for My glory, for My own sake, for Myself." This is the way God chose to do it. It is what he wants. It is the means whereby he is glorified for his grace to sinners.

---

11. Here I am following B. B. Warfield's observation that what is often called "Calvinism" is merely the biblical faith coming to full bloom. In "What is Calvinism?" he writes, "For Calvinism is just religion in its purity. We have only, therefore, to conceive of religion in its purity, and that is Calvinism" (6).

Part IV: Redemption Glorified

CONCLUSION

The Father chose some ("us") in Christ Jesus, the Son. It is these same ones for whom Christ dies. It is these same ones whom the Spirit sanctifies.

Any view which introduces disharmony into the triune God must be rejected since, as established elsewhere in this work, no one person of the Trinity ever operates "from Himself." There exists glorious harmony among the Trinity. The Father, the Son, and the Holy Spirit have a single divine intention in redemption. Therefore, while differing roles for each member of the Godhead are discernible from revelation (e.g., it is the Son who dies on the cross, not the Father or the Spirit), the work of the triune God is one work. Thus, of the above 27 options for the outworking of the work of redemption by the Trinity, all but three introduce disharmony and discord within that work. These are:

> *The Father elects none, the Son dies for none, the Spirit sanctifies none.*
> *The Father elects all, the Son dies for all, the Spirit sanctifies all.*
> *The Father elects some, the Son dies for some, the Spirit sanctifies some.*

Of these three options wherein unity is maintained, only one option is truly biblical: the Father from eternity elected some for salvation in Christ, the Son is sent by the Father to die for those chosen by the Father in him, and the Spirit sent by the Father and the Son perfectly applies the completed work of Christ to those chosen by God and sets them apart as holy unto God.

Considering the atonement in isolation, the sacrifice of Christ on the cross can be recognized for its inherent worth and infinite value. It is God dying according to his human nature. Therefore, it is of infinite worth. As such, it is sufficient not only to atone for all the sins of every person who ever lived in this world, but it is sufficient to atone for an infinite number of sins or an infinite number of people on an infinite number of worlds. Since it is God in the flesh who dies, one might even speculate that given the infinite worth of the sacrifice, it is sufficient to atone of the sins of all the fallen angels, the devil included. Again, considering the atonement in isolation can result in these speculative conclusions.

However, the work of Christ on the cross cannot be isolated from the electing work of the Father before time nor the sanctifying work of the Spirit in time. The cross of Christ and his atoning sacrifice for sin is situated within a Trinitarian framework as well as motivated by the divine intention of the Trinity aimed at the glorification of the Father, the Son, and the Holy

Spirit. Therefore, the atonement must not be considered in isolation, which renders the above-mentioned speculative conclusions moot.

Either the Trinity really saves a particular people, or the Trinity merely provides a potential salvation for a hypothetical people. The former presents the Father, the Son, and the Holy Spirit as really saving people from eternity to eternity. The latter presents the Father trying to save, the Son trying to save, and the Holy Spirit trying to save, but the entire Trinity can be and is thwarted and frustrated by the almighty will of the creature.

Those given by the Father to the Son are then drawn by the Father through the Spirit to the Son. When the Trinity determines to save, the Father, the Son, and the Holy Spirit really do save. The Father, the Son, and the Holy Spirit really do save all those whom they choose to save. This is the gospel according to the Trinity.

Atonement is the act of the triune God. Therefore, one must understand the Father's role and purpose, the Son's role and purpose, and the Holy Spirit's role and purpose. The atonement is an act designed with a specific divine intention, viz., the glorification of the triune God. The triune God glorifies himself in the redemption of sinners. It starts with the triune God in eternity. It moves through the work of the Trinity across time and space in accomplishing and applying eternal redemption to sinners. It culminates in eternity with the glorification of a particular people to the glory of the triune God. The electing act of the Father, the self-sacrificial act of the Son on the cross for his people and his continued mediation for his people as their great high priest, and the regenerating work of the Spirit in perfectly applying the completed work of Christ to the people given by the Father to Son—all of this is the consistent, harmonious, and singular work and intention of the eternal triune God as presented in Scripture.

Appendix

Against Universalism

Universalism is defined as "the notion that all intelligent, moral creatures (angels, humans, devils) will be saved in the end."[1] While this is the doctrine proper, typically what is meant is the salvation of all human beings. So Evans:

> The belief that all persons will eventually be saved and thus that no one will be eternally lost. Some universalists hold that all will be saved because of the work of Christ, but some deny the unique deity of Christ and necessity of his work for salvation in favor of a pluralistic view that sees the world's religions as equally valid. Universalism should not be confused with the view that it is possible that *some* who do not have conscious faith in Christ in this life may be saved. It also should be distinguished from annihilationism, which holds that those who are eternally lost cease to exist altogether.[2]

This appendix will identify how universalism is unbiblical. It will do so by, first, showing that universalism does not align with the overall biblical message of eternal destinies. Second, it will interact with various proof texts and demonstrate exegetically that these texts do not support universalism.

---

1. Gundry-Volf, "Universalism," 956.
2. Evans, *Pocket Dictionary*, 119. Emphasis original.

Appendix

THREE SCRIPTURAL ASSUMPTIONS OPPOSED TO UNIVERSALISM

The Scriptures assume that some *will*, not just *could*, perish. Isaiah sees rebels whose dead bodies are forever consumed by worms and fire; the rebels themselves are "an abhorrence to all flesh" (Isa 66:24). Daniel sees some of the dead who rise "to shame and everlasting contempt" (Dan 12:2). Jesus says that those who do not repent *will* "perish" (Luke 13:3, 5). Those who do not believe in Jesus will not have eternal life but will "perish" (John 3:16). Those who do not know God and do not obey the gospel of the Lord Jesus "will suffer the punishment of eternal destruction" (2 Thess 1:8–9). These are all in the indicative mood, the mood of reality.

It should be noted that "eternal destruction" points to either destruction which lasts forever (unending) or annihilation. The fact that there will be those who experience this eliminates universalism from consideration.

The Scriptures assume two ultimate destinies—one with God, the other away from God. Yahweh through Jeremiah says there are two ways: a way of life and a way of death (Jer 21:8). This is rooted in Torah, trajectories which result in life or death (Deut 30:15–20). Daniel speaks of "everlasting life" and "everlasting contempt" (12:2). Jesus himself talks about heaven and hell: the former is a place of "joy" (Matt 25:21, 23), "life" (Matt 7:14; Mark 9:45), "eternal life" (Matt 19:30), and "blessing" (Matt 25:34); the latter is a place of "darkness" (Matt 25:30), "weeping and gnashing of teeth" (Luke 13:28), "eternal fire" (Matt 18:8, 9), and "hell" (Mark 9:43, 47). Paul, while discussing the righteous judgment of God "on the day of wrath," says there is one destiny of "eternal life" and another of "wrath and fury" (Rom 2:5–8).

The Scriptures assume the final destinies are fixed postmortem. In the parable of the rich man and Lazarus, a parable with clear eschatological importance, Abraham tells the rich man, "Between us and you a great chasm has been fixed, in order that those who would pass from here to you may not be able, and none may cross from there to us" (Luke 16:26). "It is appointed for man to die once, and after that comes judgment" (Heb 9:27). Both life with God which the righteous will enjoy and the punishment of those under the curse of God are described as "eternal."

TACKLING UNIVERSALIST PROOF TEXTS

Acts 3:21

> ... whom heaven must receive until the time for restoring all the things about which God spoke by the mouth of his holy prophets long ago. (Acts 3:21)

"Restoration of all things" translates *aposkatastaseus pantōn*. *Pantōn* could be masculine or neuter, but since it is followed by *hōn* which is neuter and related grammatically to *pantōn*, then *pantōn* must be neuter. Hence, the ESV has rendered it accurately as "all things." So Oepke argues, "Grammatically [*hōn*] cannot be related to [*chronōn*] but only to [*pantōn*]. This means further that [*pantōn*] can only be neut. and not masc."[3] Gundry-Wolf astutely notes that this phrase, then, "does not denote the conversion of all persons but the 'restoration of all *things*' ... or the universal renewal of the earth."[4] Therefore, the salvation of all people is not in view in this text.

Romans 5:12–21

A universalist reading of this text sees all people in Adam being made righteous in Christ. The sin of Adam resulted in "condemnation for all people" and the act of righteousness of Christ results in "justification and life for all men" (v. 18). This is the parallel that universalists lean into.

However, while "all" is pressed into service, the term "many" is either overlooked or else equated with "all." By Adam's sin "the many were made sinners," and by Christ's obedience "the many will be made righteous" (v. 19). *Many* serves to restrict *all*. This is because Paul is contrasting two humanities: one in Adam and one in Christ. Hence a proper reading would be as follows:

> 18 Therefore, as one trespass led to condemnation for all men [viz. all people in Adam], so one act of righteousness leads to justification and life for all men [viz. all people in Christ].
>
> 19 For as by the one man's [Adam's] disobedience the many [in Adam] were made sinners, so by the one man's [Christ's] obedience the many [in Christ] will be made righteous.

---

3. *TDNT* 1:391.
4. Gundry-Volf, "Universalism," 956.

Appendix

In addition, it can be argued that "all" refers to *people from all over the world*, i.e., Jews and gentiles. This ties directly back to the thesis statement in 1:16–17, through 3:9, while incorporating the gospel, which finds all human beings condemned by the Law, but those who believe are justified (3:20–24).

Furthermore, 5:17 deepens the distinction between "those who receive the abundance of grace and the free gift of righteousness," even "the righteousness of God through the faithfulness of Jesus Christ for all who believe" (3:22), and those who have not received grace and righteousness and remain under condemnation for their sins.

Romans 11:32

> For God has consigned all to disobedience, that he may have mercy on all. (Rom 11:32)

This relates to 5:19–20: the universal condemnation is for all people in Adam; the justification to life is for all people in Christ. Further, the immediate context demonstrates that Paul has people groups in mind, viz., Jews and gentiles. Hence, "that he may have mercy in all" speaks to God having mercy on all people, Jews first and then gentiles, not God *will* show mercy on all, in some universalist way. God's mercy is available to all people; that is, it is *sufficient* for all people, but *efficient* only for the obedient in Christ. God may/might show mercy on all if they believe in Christ, repent, and obey the gospel.

1 Corinthians 15:22, 28

> For as in Adam all die, so also in Christ shall all be made alive. (1 Cor 15:22)

The universalist fails to read this text in context: the very next verse affirms a distinction, recognizing "those who belong to Christ" (v. 23), which assumes there are those who are outside of Christ. Hence, the asymmetrical parallelism is evident.

> When all things are subjected to him, then the Son himself will also be subjected to him who put all things in subjection under him, that God may be all in all. (1 Cor 15:28)

Against Universalism

"All things" brought into subjection to Christ does not mean universal salvation. Once again, context torpedoes the universalist. There are clear allusions to Ps 110, as Christ is reigning now in the midst of his enemies, bringing all of his enemies into subjection, "destroying every rule and every authority and power" (v. 24). This includes the last enemy, Death (v. 26). Therefore, God being all in all does not mean universal salvation, but the final glorification of the triune God in bringing "those who belong to Christ" to glory.

Philippians 2:10–11

> ... so that at the name of Jesus every knee should bow, in heaven and on earth and under the earth, and every tongue confess that Jesus Christ is Lord, to the glory of God the Father. (Phil 2:10–11)

It is assumed the confession of "every tongue" is a saving confession. Rather, the eschatological picture portrayed here is the universal recognition of Christ as Lord to the salvation of his people (the saints of God are exhorted to "work out your own salvation," [v. 12] and that God is at work for his good pleasure in them [v. 13]) but to the condemnation of his enemies (cf. 3:18). Further, the contrast between "enemies of the cross" whose "end is destruction" is contrasted with citizens of the kingdom who await their Savior from heaven (3:19–20).

2 Corinthians 5:19

> ... that is, in Christ *God was reconciling the world to himself*, not counting their trespasses against them, and entrusting to us the message of reconciliation. (2 Cor 5:19)

Again, the assumption is that "world" means "every single person who ever lived." However, the following phrase, "not counting their trespasses against them," is descriptive of Christians. Indeed, in the preceding verse, Paul had just written, "[God] through Christ reconciled us to Himself," i.e., Christians, Paul included. Further, the message of reconciliation goes forth from the church: "Be reconciled to God!" (v. 20).

Appendix

Colossians 1:20

> ... and *through him to reconcile to himself all things*, whether on earth or in heaven, making peace by the blood of his cross. (Col 1:20)

Here is where universalism proper dwells: the complete reconciliation of everything, all beings—human and angelic—things "on earth or in heaven." The context is clearly in reference to the atonement since it is "by the blood of [Jesus'] cross" whereby peace is made.

In addition, the context also particularizes this reconciliation. The next verse sees Paul addressing these Christians as those who were "once alienated and hostile in mind, doing evil deeds" but "now reconciled" by God through the death of Christ. It is this particularity which militates against universalism. Furthermore, continued, steadfast faith in Christ is required, as is evident in verse 23. Without faith, there is no reconciliation.

Others have also pointed to the nature of reconciliation. One is either reconciled to Christ by means of salvation for peace, or one remains unreconciled and at war ("hostile"), primed for subjection to the Lord.

Ephesians 1:10

> ... as a plan for the fullness of time, *to unite all things in him*, things in heaven and things on earth. (Eph 1:10)

This text falls prey to the same critique as Col 1:20. Further, the larger context (v. 3–14) is rife with particularity, which militates against the universalist ("we" and "us" language abounds).

Leaving those to the side, though, another troubling shortcoming of the universalist reading of this text is that the unification of all things in Christ is a past tense event. God accomplished his plan in "the fullness of time" through the exaltation of Christ. Therefore, all things are under Christ's feet; Christ is head over all things to the church (1:22). Indeed, this is one reason why God can work all things according to the counsel of his will (1:11). Hence, this is not an eschatological context.

Close reading of each of these texts in their given context eliminates the confusion and even contradiction that universalism introduces. Universalism fails to attain through exegesis of the Scriptures. It is wholly unbiblical and should be rejected on exegetical grounds.

"BUT I'M JUST A HOPEFUL UNIVERSALIST"

Since the case cannot be made objectively through careful exegesis of the text, a more subjective approach to Scripture might be taken. It may be argued that hell is too awful to contemplate or that it is somehow unbecoming of holy deity. Therefore, something nicer, cleaner is offered: universalism. Universalism is more user friendly and pastorally sensitive. In this way the phrase "hopeful universalist" is born.

It needs to be pointed out that "hopeful" as it is used in the phrase "hopeful universalist" is not biblical hope. Biblical hope is not wishful thinking. In addition, assuming a biblical definition of hope, then our hope ought to be that "the Judge of all the earth will do what is just" according to the holy counsel of his will.

Now, if one wants to say, "The very clear, plain teaching of Scripture says eternal conscious punishment, but I sure hope I have misunderstood this very clear and plain teaching so that somehow everyone is saved," well, that's an altogether different discussion. But that usually isn't what is being said or advocated.

THE ANALOGY OF FAITH AND UNIVERSALISM

Universalism leans onto challenging phrases in select verses of Scripture as the primary source of their doctrine. However, the clear passages of Scripture ought to be used to illuminate these more obscure or vague texts.

The only infallible tool for interpreting Scripture is Scripture itself. We believe in the perspicuity of Scripture, that the revelation is clear. There is general clarity in all Scripture, spoken by God so that creatures could understand. At the same time, we hold that not all individual texts of Scripture are equally clear. Scripture is a perfectly clear revelation from the infinite God to finite humans. But even Peter acknowledged that some passages (e.g., from Paul) are harder to understand than others.

So we allow the more easily interpreted passages to interpret the more difficult to understand passages. It is not that we have a bullpen of passages for our pet doctrine and then everything else gets filtered through that matrix of verses. Rather, we let easy to understand passages interpret more difficult passages.

Further, we do not have a canon within a canon, a matrix of verses which have priority over other passages. Rather, we hold that all Scripture

Appendix

holds together consistently, and therefore all Scripture must be brought to bear on the interpretation of a particular text (i.e., not isolating passages from the rest of Scripture).

Bibliography

Allen, David L. *Hebrews*. The New American Commentary. Nashville: B & H, 2010.
Allen, R. Michael. *Karl Barth's Church Dogmatics: An Introduction and Reader*. London, New York: T & T Clark, 2012.
Ambrose of Milan. "Three Books of St. Ambrose on the Holy Spirit." In *St. Ambrose: Select Works and Letters*. Edited by Philip Schaff and Henry Wace. Translated by H. de Romestin, E. de Romestin, and H. T. F. Duckworth. Vol. 10 of *A Select Library of the Nicene and Post-Nicene Fathers of the Christian Church, Second Series*. New York: Christian Literature Company, 1896.
Arnold, Clinton E. *Ephesians*. Zondervan Exegetical Commentary on the New Testament. Grand Rapids: Zondervan, 2010.
Arndt, William, et al. *A Greek-English Lexicon of the New Testament and Other Early Christian Literature*. Chicago: University of Chicago Press, 2000.
Barth, Karl. *Church Dogmatics*. Vol. II.2. Peabody, MA: Hendrickson, 2010.
Bell, Rob. *Love Wins*. New York: HarperOne, 2011.
Boice, James Montgomery. *Foundations of the Christian Faith: A Comprehensive & Readable Theology*. Downers Grove, IL: InterVarsity, 1986.
Boyd, Gregory A. *God of the Possible: A Biblical Introduction to the Open View of God*. Grand Rapids: Baker, 2000.
Brents, T. W. *Gospel Sermons*. Nashville: McQuiddy, 1918.
———. *The Gospel Plan of Salvation*. 16th ed. Nashville: Gospel Advocate Company, 1977.
Camp, Franklin. *The Work of the Holy Spirit in Redemption*. Bowling Green, KY: Guardian of Truth Foundation, 1972.
Campbell, Alexander. *The Christian System*. 2nd ed. Pittsburg: Forrester & Campbell, 1837.
Campbell, Travis James. *The Wonderful Decree: Reconciling Sovereign Election and Universal Benevolence*. Bellingham, WA: Lexham, 2020.
Carter, Kelly D. *The Trinity in the Stone-Campbell Movement*. Abilene, TX: ACU Press, 2015.
Carson, D. A. *The Gospel according to John*. The Pillar New Testament Commentary. Grand Rapids: Eerdmans, 1991.
Clarke, Adam. *Clarke's Commentary*. New York: Abingdon, n.d.

Bibliography

Coffman, James Burton. "Commentary on 2 Thessalonians." Coffman's Commentaries on the Bible. Abilene, Texas: Abilene Christian University Press, 1983–99. https://www.studylight.org/commentaries/eng/bcc/2-thessalonians-2.html.

———. "Commentary on 2 Timothy 1." Coffman's Commentary on the Bible. Abilene, TX: Abilene Christian University Press, n.d. https://www.studylight.org/commentaries/eng/bcc/2-timothy-1.html.

———. "Commentary on John 6." Coffman's Commentary on the Bible. Abilene, TX: Abilene Christian University Press, 1996. https://www.studylight.org/commentaries/eng/bcc/john-6.html.

———. "Commentary on Romans 8." Coffman's Commentaries on the Bible. Abilene, TX: Abilene Christian University Press, n.d. https://www.studylight.org/commentaries/eng/bcc/romans-8.html.

Dunn, James D. G. *Romans 1–8*. Vol. 38a. Word Biblical Commentary. Dallas: Word, 1988.

Eadie, John. *A Commentary on the Greek Text of the Epistle of Paul to the Ephesians*. Ed. W. Young. Edinburgh: T & T Clark, 1883.

Edwards, Jonathan. *Heaven Is a World of Love*. Crossway Short Classics Series. Wheaton, IL: Crossway, 2020.

———. *The End for Which God Created the World*. Ed. John Piper. *God's Passion for His Glory*. Wheaton, IL: Crossway, 1998.

Erickson, Millard J. *Making Sense of the Trinity*. Grand Rapids: Baker Academic, 2000.

Evans, C. Stephen. *Pocket Dictionary of Apologetics & Philosophy of Religion*. Downers Grove, IL: InterVarsity, 2002.

Feinberg, John S. *No One Like Him*. Wheaton, IL: Crossway, 2001.

Gibson, Jonathan. "The Glorious, Indivisible, Trinitarian Work of God in Christ." In *From Heaven He Came and Sought Her*, eds. David Gibson and Jonathan Gibson, 331–74. Wheaton, IL: Crossway, 2013.

Green, Gene L. *The Letters to the Thessalonians*. Pillar New Testament Commentary. Grand Rapids: Eerdmans, 2002.

Grudem, Wayne. *1 Peter*. Vol 17. Tyndale New Testament Commentaries. Grand Rapids: Eerdmans, 1988.

Gould, Marcus T. C. *A Debate Between Rev. A. Campbell and Rev. N. L. Rice on the Subject, Actions, Design, and Administrator of Christian Baptism*. Jacksonville, IL: C. D. Roberts, 1857.

Gundry-Volf, Judith M. "Universalism." In *Dictionary of Paul and His Letters*, edited by Gerald F. Hawthorne, Ralph P. Martin, and Daniel G. Reid, 956–61. Downers Grove, IL: InterVarsity, 1993.

Hendriksen, William, and Simon J. Kistemaker. *Exposition of Galatians*. Vol. 8. New Testament Commentary. Grand Rapids: Baker Book House, 1953–2001.

Hill, Gerald. "2 Timothy." *Contending for the Faith Commentary*. Edited by Joe Norton. Yukon, OK: Contending for the Faith, 2021. https://www.studylight.org/commentaries/eng/ctf/2-timothy-1.html.

Hoyt, Samuel L. *The Judgment Seat of Christ*. Rev. Ed. Duluth, MN: Grace Gospel, 2015.

Jackson, Wayne. "The Praying to Jesus Controversy." *Christian Courier* (Aug. 2010) 16–29.

Keil, Carl Friedrich, and Franz Delitzsch. *Commentary on the Old Testament*. Vol. 5. Peabody, MA: Hendrickson, 1996.

Köstenberger, Andreas J. "John." *Commentary on the New Testament Use of the Old Testament*. Edited by G. K. Beale and D. A. Carson. Grand Rapids: Baker Academic, 2007.

Bibliography

Kruse, Colin G. *John: An Introduction and Commentary.* Edited by Eckhard J. Schnabel. 2nd ed. Vol. 4. Tyndale New Testament Commentaries. London: InterVarsity, 2017.

Kruse, Colin G. *Paul's Letter to the Romans.* Edited by D. A. Carson. Pillar New Testament Commentary. Grand Rapids: Eerdmans, 2012.

Lard, Moses E. *Commentary on Romans.* Delight, AR: Gospel Light, n.d.

Lenski, R. C. H. *The Interpretation of St. John's Gospel.* Minneapolis: Augsburg, 1961.

———. *The Interpretation of St. Paul's Epistle to the Romans.* Columbus, OH: Lutheran Book Concern, 1936.

———. *The Interpretation of St. Paul's Epistles to the Galatians, to the Ephesians and to the Philippians.* Columbus, OH: Lutheran Book Concern, 1937.

Lipscomb, David. *A Commentary on the Gospel of John.* Edited by C. E. W. Dorris. Nashville: Gospel Advocate, 1956.

Lloyd-Jones, D. Martyn. *Romans: An Exposition of Chapters 3.20–24.25.* Grand Rapids: Zondervan, 1970.

Long, Fredrick J. *Kairos: A Beginning Greek Grammar.* Mishawaka, IN: Fredrick J. Long, 2005.

Louw, Johannes P., and Eugene Albert Nida. *Greek-English Lexicon of the New Testament: Based on Semantic Domains.* Vol. 1. New York: United Bible Societies, 1996.

Malone, Avon. *The Purpose and the People.* Nashville: 21st Century Christian, 1994.

McRaney, Will. *The Art of Personal Evangelism: Sharing Jesus in a Changing Culture.* Nashville: Broadman & Holman, 2003.

Miller, Stephen R. *Daniel.* Vol. 18. New American Commentary. Nashville: B & H, 1994.

Moffitt, David M. *Rethinking the Atonement: New Perspectives on Jesus's Death, Resurrection, and Ascension.* Grand Rapids: Baker Academic, 2022.

Moo, Douglas. *The Epistle to the Romans.* New International Commentary on the New Testament. Grand Rapids: Eerdmans, 1996.

Morris, Leon. *The Apostolic Preaching of the Cross.* 3rd ed. Grand Rapids: Eerdmans, 1965.

———. *The Epistle to the Romans.* Pillar New Testament Commentary. Grand Rapids: Eerdmans, 1988.

Mounce, Robert H. *The Book of Revelation.* New International Commentary of the New Testament. Rev. Ed. Grand Rapids: Eerdmans, 1998.

Murray, John. *Redemption Accomplished and Applied.* Grand Rapids: Eerdmans, 2015.

Oepke, Albrecht. "Ἀποκαθίστημι, Ἀποκατάστασις." In *Theological Dictionary of the New Testament.* Vol. 1. Edited by Gerhard Kittel, Geoffrey W. Bromiley, and Gerhard Friedrich. Grand Rapids: Eerdmans, 1964.

Osburn, Glen. "Ephesians." *Contending for the Faith Commentary.* Edited by Charles Bailey. Yukon, OK: Contending for the Faith, 1997. https://www.studylight.org/commentaries/eng/ctf/ephesians-1.html.

Owen, John. *An Exposition of the Epistle to the Hebrews.* Vol. 20. Edited by W. H. Goold. Works of John Owen. Edinburgh: Johnstone and Hunter, 1854.

———. *The Works of John Owen.* Edited by William H. Goold. Vol. 2. Edinburgh: T & T Clark, n.d.

Peterson, Robert A. *Salvation Applied by the Spirit: Union with Christ.* Wheaton, IL: Crossway, 2015.

Pink, Arthur W. *Exposition of the Gospel of John.* Grand Rapids: Zondervan, 1945.

Robertson, A. T. *A Grammar of the Greek New Testament in the Light of Historical Research.* Logos Bible Software, 2006.

Ryle, J. C. *Expository Thoughts on the Gospels.* Vol 3. Grand Rapids: Baker, 2007.

Bibliography

Sanders, Fred. *The Triune God*. Edited by Michael Allen and Scott R. Swain. New Studies in Dogmatics. Grand Rapids: Zondervan, 2016.

Scheurers, Timothy. "An Evaluation of Some Aspects of Karl Barth's Doctrine of Election." *Mid-America Journal of Theology* 22 (2011) 161–73.

Schreiner, Thomas R. *1, 2 Peter, Jude*. Vol. 37 of *The New American Commentary*. Nashville: Broadman & Holman, 2003.

———. *Romans*. Baker Exegetical Commentary on the New Testament. Grand Rapids: Baker, 1998.

Sproul, R. C. *Chosen by God*. Wheaton, IL: Tyndale House, 1986.

Stott, John R. W. *The Cross of Christ*. Downers Grove, IL: IVP, 2006.

Taylor, Jr., Robert. *The Bible Doctrine of the Holy Spirit*. Abilene, TX: Quality, 1996.

Thayer, Joseph Henry. *A Greek-English Lexicon of the New Testament: Being Grimm's Wilke's Clavis Novi Testamenti*. New York: Harper & Brothers, 1889.

Torrance, Thomas F. *The Trinitarian Faith: The Evangelical Theology of the Ancient Catholic Church*. 2nd ed. The Cornerstones Series. New York: Bloomsbury T & T Clark, 2016.

Van Til, Cornelius. *Christianity and Barthianism*. Grand Rapids: Baker, 1962.

Wallace, Daniel B. *Greek Grammar Beyond the Basics*. Grand Rapids: Zondervan, 1996.

Ware, Bruce. "Christ's Atonement: A Work of the Trinity." In *Jesus in Trinitarian Perspective*, edited by Fred Sanders and Klaus Issler, 156–88. Nashville: B & H Academic, 2007.

Warfield, B. B. "Trinity." In *The International Bible Standard Bible Encyclopedia*, edited by James Orr, 3012–22. Grand Rapids: Eerdmans, 1939.

———. "What is Calvinism?" In *Selected Shorter Writings of Benjamin B. Warfield*. Vol. 1. Edited by John E. Meeter. Nutley, NJ: P & R, 1970.

White, James R. *Drawn by the Father*. Lindenhurst, NY: Great Christian, 2000.

———. *The Forgotten Trinity*. Rev. ed. Minneapolis: Bethany House, 2019.

———. *The God Who Justifies*. Minneapolis: Bethany House, 2011.

———. *The Potter's Freedom*. Amityville, NY: Calvary, 2000.

Zaspel, Fred G. *The Theology of B. B. Warfield: A Systematic Summary*. Wheaton, IL: Crossway, 2010.

Scripture Index

Genesis

5:3	69
6:5	73
8:1	32
8:21	73
12:2	62n20
12:3	62n21, 99
13:6	62n20
15:6	99
17:4	62n20
18:18	62n20, n21
22:17	62n20
22:18	62n21

Exodus

2:24	32
17:3	86n12
32	30
32:32	30, 33
33:19	145
34:7	61

Leviticus

4:4–5	44
4:15–16	44
16	46
16:5	46
16:9	46
16:11	44, 46
16:14	44
16:15–16	43
16:15	44
17:11	53
18:5	99

Numbers

14:27	86n12
14:29	86n12
19	46
19:9	46

Deuteronomy

4:32–34	121
6:4	1
7:6–8	23
7:8	23
9:5–6	23
9:6	23
21:23	99
27:26	99
30:15–20	158
32:4	145

Joshua

24:15	121

Scripture Index

Ezra
6:1	30

Esther
6:1	30

Job
5:12	103
42:2	22

Psalms
2:3–4	103
2:9	50
4:3	153
14:3	72, 74
23:3	94n28
25:9	95
31:5	47
33:10–11	103
33:10	22
33:11	22
40:6	42
53:1	74
56:8	30
60	48
60:1–3	48
65:7	34n8
69:14	31
69:18	31
69:19	31
69:20–27	31
69:28	31
79:9	103, 153
90:2	59
104	67
104:30	67
106:8	103
110	161
139:16	30
143:10	95
147:19–20	121

Proverbs
1:7	72
1:22	72
16:9	103
19:21	103
21:30	103
26:12	72

Ecclesiastes
7:20	74
7:29	69
9:3	73

Isaiah
4:3	35
14:24	103
14:27	104, 113
17:12	34n8
43:11	153
43:21	153
46:10	113
48:11	153
49:2	50
51:2	121
52:17	49n3
52:22	49n3
53	91
53:11	91
53:12	91
53:13	91
54	91
54:1	91
54:3	91
54:5	91
54:7	91
54:8a	91
54:8b	91
54:11	91
54:13	91
57:20	34n8
62:11	50, 51
63:1–6	50
63:2	50n5
63:3	50n5
63:3a	50
63:3b	50
63:8	51
63:10	51
63:10	51
64:10	74
66:24	158

Scripture Index

Jeremiah

4:22	72
6:23	34n8
10:14	72
17:9	73
21:8	158
25:15–17	49n3
31:3	59
49:23	34n8
51:36	34n8
51:42	34n8

Ezekiel

11:19	73
26:3	34n8
36:26	73, 101, 122
36:27	122

Daniel

4:34–35	103
7:2–3	34n8
7:9–10	34
12:1	32
12:2	158

Hosea

11:7	73

Habakkuk

2:4	99

Zechariah

7:12	73

Malachi

1:14	32
1:17	32

Matthew

3:16–17	2
4:1	2
6:1–18	75n12
7:14	158
8:22	72
18:8	158
18:9	158
19:30	158
21:33–44	49n4
21:41	49
22:14	121
25:21	158
25:23	158
25:30	158
26:46	47
27:52–53	126, 127, 128
28:19	3

Mark

7:21	73
7:23	73
9:43	158
9:45	158
9:47	158
12:1–12	49n4
14:58	42

Luke

1:31	42
1:35	42
9:35	140
10:20	35
13:3	158
13:5	158
13:28	158
14:16	121
15:24	72
15:32	72
16:26	158
20:9–18	49n4
20:16	49
23:46	47

John

1:1	17
1:11	77
1:14	93
1:18	92
1:18b	93
1:18c	93
3:16	53, 83, 158

Scripture Index

John (*cont.*)

3:19	73
3:35	7
3:30	49
3:36	49, 57, 58
4:34	42, 81
4:42	151
5:19	8, 68, 81
5:19b	68
5:21	68
5:24	33
5:29	83
5:30	19
5:37	92
6	76, 83, 95
6:1–34	77
6:1–15	76
6:4	77
6:15	76
6:16–21	76
6:22–24	77
6:26	77
6:29	77
6:30	77
6:31	77
6:32	77
6:33	77
6:34	77
6:35	77, 78
6:36	77, 79, 96
6:37	77, 80, 90, 93
6:38	8, 19, 81, 85, 131, 142
6:39–40	84
6:39	77, 80, 82, 84, 85, 93
6:39b	85
6:40	82, 83, 84, 93, 95
6:41–43	85
6:41	86n12
6:44–45	92
6:44	86, 88, 90, 92, 93, 97n31
6:45	88, 89, 91, 92, 93, 94
6:46	92, 93
6:47	93, 95
6:51	95
6:54	95
6:58	95
6:59	76
6:60–61	96
6:63	67, 95
6:64	96
6:65	77, 90, 96, 97n31
6:66	76, 78
6:68	95
8:28	9
8:28b	94
8:29	8
8:47	79
8:54	18
10:17–18	131
10:26	79
10:38	8
11:4	18
11:51–52	58
12:29	61
12:32	88
12:50	8
13:18	141
13:31	9
13:31–32	18
14:10	8
14:13	18
14:16	8, 9, 98
14:17	98
14:23	98, 100
14:26	94
16:12	9
16:13	8, 68, 94, 95, 152
16:13b	9
16:14	9
16:14b-15	9
16:13–15	8, 18n1
17	17, 82, 83
17:1	18
17:3	1
17:4	9, 18, 61, 81
17:5	9, 15, 17, 130
17:11	130
17:13	130
17:17	149
17:20	20, 130
17:21	8
17:22	20, 82n5

Scripture Index

17:23-24	36
17:23b-24	20, 60
17:23	59, 120
17:23b	20
17:24	15, 18, 20, 59, 82, 90, 129
18:10	88
18:37	79
19:30	43
21:6	88, 89
21:11	88

Acts

1:9	130
2:23	119
2:33	100
2:38	98
3:21	159
5:3	1
5:4	1
14:22	111
16:14	122
17:28	111
26:5	13, 119
26:18	73

Romans

1:1	121
1:7	121
1:16-17	56, 160
1:18	53, 55, 72
1:19	127
1:21	72, 73, 101
1:22	72
1:24	72
1:25	72
1:26	73
1:28	72
1:30	74, 87
2:5-8	158
2:19	73
3:9	55, 160
3:10	74
3:11	72, 74, 87
3:12	74
3:19-20	53
3:20-24	160
3:20	54
3:21-31	54
3:21	54
3:22	56, 160
3:23	55
3:24-25	53, 54
3:25	53, 55
3:26	56
3:28	56
5:6-8	59
5:8	142
5:10	87
5:12-20	159
5:12	34, 71
5:14	34, 71
5:17	71, 160
5:18	159
5:19-20	160
5:19	159
5:21	34, 71
7:24	109
8	109, 124
8:1	109
8:2	67
8:3-9	109
8:7-8	109
8:7	59, 74
8:9	109, 146
8:10	67, 109
8:10a	109
8:11	109
8:12-16	110
8:13	110
8:14	110, 146
8:15	102, 110
8:15b	110
8:16-17	110
8:16	111
8:17	111, 124, 125, 126
8:18	111, 124, 125, 126
8:26	120, 122
8:27	128
8:28-30	109, 116, 117, 118
8:28	28, 113, 116, 117, 120, 121, 122, 124
8:29-30	26, 113, 116, 123, 126, 127, 128
8:29	115, 123, 128

Scripture Index

Romans (cont.)

8:30	121, 122, 124, 125, 126
8:31	120, 122, 123
8:32	122, 128
8:33	123
9:2	72
9:11	28
9:15	145
9:18	61
9:19–24	147
11:2	119
11:32	127, 160
11:33	145
15:16	144
16	120

1 Corinthians

1:19	22
1:20	127
2:14	69, 70
3:16–17	98
3:19	72
6:11	99
6:19	98
15:22	160
15:24	161
15:26	161
15:28	160

2 Corinthians

3:3	67
3:6	67
3:17	67
3:18	123
4:4	6, 39
4:6	6, 39
5:19	161
5:20	161
9:7	72

Galatians

2:20	63
3–4	99
3:1–5	99
3:2	99
3:6–22	100n2
3:6–14	99
3:8	121
3:9	100n2
3:14	62
3:15–22	99
3:16	62
3:22	99, 100n2
3:23—4:7	99
3:23	100n2
3:29	62
4:1–7	100
4:3	100
4:4–5	11
4:4	100, 101
4:5	100, 102
4:5b	100
4:6	11, 100

Ephesians

1	27
1:1	22, 23, 26
1:2	21
1:3–14	162
1:4–5	15, 21, 25, 60
1:4	11, 36, 137, 141
1:5	22
1:5b	21
1:6	107, 153
1:10	162
1:11	22, 28, 162
1:12	107, 153
1:14	107, 153
1:18	122
1:22	162
2:1	71
2:3	146
2:4	148
2:5	71
2:9	145
2.12	21
3:11	28
4:6	1
4:17	72
4:18	72, 73, 101
4:19	101
4:22	73

Scripture Index

4:30	51	1:8	28
6:21	22	1:9	15, 28, 36
		1:10	28
Philippians		2:19	32, 83, 127
2:10–11	161	3:2–4	73
2:12	161	3:8	72
2:13	161		
3:18	161	**Titus**	
3:19–20	161	1:2	15
4	33	3:3	73
4:3	33	3:5	23, 145
Colossians		**Hebrews**	
1:20	162	1:2	93
1:21	74	2:10	44, 61, 62
1:23	162	2:11	45, 62
2:13	71	2:12	62
2:14–15	44	2:13	44, 45, 62
2:20	63	2:13b	20, 45
		2:14	60
1 Thessalonians		2:15	60
1:3–5	103	2:16	45, 60, 62
1:4	103	2:17	53, 60, 62
1:5	123	3:12	73, 101
2:16	127	4:13	119
5:23	99, 102	4:15	61
		4:15b	61
		5:9	46
2 Thessalonians		7:25	44, 45
1:1	102, 103	7:26	61
1:3	102	7:27	43
1:8–9	158	8:1	130
2:1	102	8:2	44
2:10	104	9	41
2:12	104	9:1–10	41
2:13–14	102	9:7	43, 46
2:13	14, 103, 104	9:8	41
2:16	102	9:11–14	41
		9:11b	42
1 Timothy		9:12	43
5:6	72	9:13–14	45
6:13	95	9:13	45
		9:14–15	62
2 Timothy		9:14	46
		9:15	45, 47
1:8–10	27	9:24	44

Scripture Index

Hebrews (*cont.*)

9:27	158
9:28	45
10:3	46
10:5	42
10:12	43, 44

James

2:6	89

1 Peter

1:1–2	12
1:2	13, 119
1:18	72
1:20	13, 39, 119
2:9	122
3:18	144
4:1	111

2 Peter

3:17	13, 119

1 John

1:7	59
1:8	56, 58
1:10	56, 58
2:1–2	56, 58
2:2	53, 58
2:11	73
3:2	130
3:14	72
3:20	119
4:9–10	59
4:10	53
4:14	151
5:20	1

Revelation

3:5	33, 35
5:6	50
5:9	37, 45, 121
5:12–13	50
6:15–17	50
7:17	94
13:6	36
13:7–8	36
13:7	36
13:8	16, 35, 36, 37
17:8	16, 35, 36, 37
19:13	50n5
19:15	50
20:11–15	33
20:12	33, 35
20:13	33
20:13a	34
20:13b	34
20:15	35, 57
21:27	36

www.ingramcontent.com/pod-product-compliance
Lightning Source LLC
Chambersburg PA
CBHW071450150426
43191CB00008B/1302